SUPERHEDGING

SUPERHEDGING

by

Thomas C. Noddings

Probus Publishing   •   Chicago, Illinois 60606

dovetail; the former make provocative statements and get their names publicized, while the latter get dramatic stories to help sell advertising space. Any such statements are probably worthless for the very reason that got them into the media.

Worthless information of another kind is propagated by many market advisory services. Publishers of newletters are likely to be more concerned with their subscription renewal rate than with accuracy (do you blame them?). Thus, most advisory services simply echo their readers' current hopes and fears.

Still another variety of dubious investment information and advice comes from the brokerage community. Here the purpose is to increase portfolio activity, so we have the immense outpouring of opinions, bulletins, recommendations, figures, reports, and forecasts issuing from Wall Street. Their value, if any, is short-lived by design.

Aside from the difficulty in acquiring a sound investment education, the modern investor has a new problem: changes in the securities markets themselves. Once upon a time, these markets were auctions that responded to millions of individual buyers and sellers. No longer, though. Today, they're under the control of a few hundred large institutions.

So—lacking a real investment education, caught up in an atmosphere of biased advice, overloaded with information, and trampled by the institutions—it's no wonder most people lose money in the stock market.

But it doesn't have to be that way.

A few individuals do manage to educate themselves. Calmly and confidently, they bypass all gratuitous advice and information, whether it comes from self-styled experts, advisory services, or the brokerage industry. The institutions are too big to be bypassed, of course, but knowledgeable investors don't even try. Instead, they beat the giants on their own turf by exploiting their weaknesses: their enormous size, their legal constraints, and their need to dress up quarterly reports. The investors I speak of take impressive profits out of Wall Street—year after year—while keeping their risk prudently low at all times. Furthermore, they accomplish all this with only a reasonable investment of time. Their secret? The advanced investment strategies they use.

This book will teach *you* how to use those strategies.

If you're about to discover its author for the first time, get ready for some straight talk. Tom Noddings promises no short cuts to wealth; there isn't a single hot tip in this entire volume. But "convertible securities," "hedging," and "long-term capital gains" are endearing concepts, in a capitalistic sort of way, and if you're an experienced investor you'll learn how to use them more effectively in these pages.

More than that, you'll find the book to be a revelation of stock market technique and philosophy, a piece of The Truth. Soundly based on original research, it won't let you shrug your shoulders and walk away. Noddings writes in a quiet voice—which makes his logic all the more devastating—but he cuts through half-baked conclusions and investment nonsense as with a surgeon's scalpel. Between these covers, an entire herd of sacred cows is neatly disposed of.

Meanwhile, in richly-detailed chapters the author explains contemporary investing step by step, more logically than anyone else who's written about it. There aren't many writers who are prolific, yet manage to maintain a consistently high standard. Noddings is one of the few who do, which is why his work always get an especially warm welcome from sophisticated investors. A seasoned engineer, he's been trained to look, question and study. Here he applies this training, enhanced by a thinking mind, to the stock market. You'll be astonished and delighted by his investment perceptions. Once again, he demonstrates that investing is strange, funny, and—above all—comprehensible.

The crucial test of the stock market professional is his ability to bring it all together where it counts: in the real world. Theories are fine, truths are beautiful, but without application they're esthetic and sterile. On the other hand, proven investment strategies are fascinating, and Tom Noddings has tested his strategies with millions of dollars of cold cash in the hot forge of the market.

Are you still wondering whether this book is any different from others on the subject? If so, you can stop right now; I guarantee you'll never look at stocks and bonds in the same way again after you finish it.

Earl Zazove

INTRODUCTION TO HEDGING

Hedging means different things to different people. Farmers, for example, may hedge their unharvested crops against declining prices by selling grain futures short; exporters may deal in financial futures to hedge later deliveries against fluctuating currency values. These are protective strategies designed to reduce business risks, not to achieve additional profits.

The subject of this book is hedging in the equity markets. By my definition, equity hedging involves putting on positions in stock-market-related securities that both reduce risk and achieve higher risk-adjusted rates of return than are available elsewhere. Investors who can sell their securities today, unlike farmers and exporters, have easier ways to achieve risk reduction other than the use of hedging tactics—they can immediately shift from stocks to cash. *Equity hedging must compensate for the extra time and expense through higher returns.*

Contrary to the belief that all markets are efficiently priced, above-average investment returns can be achieved by taking advantage of under- or overvalued opportunities in *stock-market-related* instruments. Pockets of pricing inefficiencies, unattractive to large institutional money managers because of limited liquidity, can be found in both convertible securities and listed options.

When I use the terms "undervalued" and "overvalued," or "underpriced" and "overpriced," I am referring to mathematical relationships—not to someone's opinion of a security or its underlying common stock. Fundamental and technical analysis may play important roles in conventional portfolio management, but they take a distant back seat in most hedging strategies.

This chapter provides an overview of profitable hedging strategies, starting with the more common risk-reduction tactics involving common stock and call options.

HEDGING NORMALLY VALUED SECURITIES

Others usually define hedging more broadly than I do; they might include any related positions—even those holding no promise for gain. This broader definition may include tax deferral and other short-term trading tactics, as well as ill-advised, long-term strategies involving normally valued (fairly valued) securities. As an example of the former, consider an investor holding a profitable position in XYZ stock who is ready to take profits in July, but wishes to defer them until the following year for tax savings. This investor might establish a "hedge" by executing a short sale against the stock he owns.

Table 1 illustrates the risk-reward characteristics of a short-against-the-box "hedge" executed in July, and held for six months until closeout in January. I assumed 100 shares of stock trading at $20 and paying a $.10-per-share quarterly dividend.

As shown by Table 1, this tax-deferral strategy doesn't offer any opportunity for profit or loss, no matter how far the stock might advance or decline over the six months. Were it not for the desired tax savings, it would make no economic sense at all; an outright sale in July would release the funds for other investments. As a trading tactic, the short-against-the-box "hedge" would make even less sense for someone who turned bearish on the market. A bearish trader would be better off selling his stock and placing the proceeds in money market instruments until he chose to reenter the stock market.

A better alternative than shorting against the box for both investors, if it were available, might be the sale of a fairly valued, in-the-money call option.

Table 1. Selling stock short-against-the-box

	*Stock Price in Six Months**		
	$ 5	$ 20	$ 40
Profit or (loss) on long stock	(1500)	0	2000
Profit or (loss) on short stock	1500	0	(2000)
Dividends received on long stock	20	20	20
Dividends paid on short stock	(20)	(20)	(20)
Total profit or (loss)	0	0	0
Six-month return on $2,000 investment	0%	0%	0%

*100 shares at $20, yielding $.10 quarterly

Let's assume that a six-month call, having a $15 exercise price, was trading at $6 ($600 for each 100 shares). Table 2 illustrates a covered writing position held for six months.

Unlike the short-against-the box maneuver, covered call writing usually offers profit opportunity in the form of any premium received above the call's intrinsic value ($100), stock dividends ($20), and interest earned on investing the call option premium in money-market instruments (10 percent annually = 5 percent of $600 for six months, or $30). Assuming the stock ends up at or above the call's $15 exercise price, a $150 total return would be earned for the six-month period. This equals 7.5 percent of the $2,000 common-stock value, or 15 percent annualized (compared to our 10 percent assumption for money-market rates of return). As an offset to the earnings potential above money market rates, covered writing does involve risk. If the stock plummets to $5, for instance, an $850 loss would result (−85 percent annualized).

Risk could be further reduced if a *deep* in-the-money call were available. Table 3 presents risk-reward calculations, assuming the sale of a six-month call having a $10 strike price and trading at $10.50. If the stock ends up at any price above $10, the six-month return of 6 percent (12 percent annualized) slightly exceeds the prevailing 10 percent Treasury bill rate. A stock price decline to $5 would lose $380 (−38 percent annualized).

Although the sale of in-the-money covered call options, as in the examples, should earn above-market rates of return most of the time, excess profits are

---

Table 2. Selling in-the-money covered call options

	Prices in Six Months			
Stock*	$ 5	$ 15	$ 20	$ 40
Call†	0	0	5	25
Profit or (loss) on stock	(1500)	(500)	0	2000
Profit or (loss) on call	600	600	100	(1900)
Dividends received	20	20	20	20
T-bill interest on $600	30	30	30	30
Total profit or (loss)	(850)	150	150	150
Six-month return on $2,000 investment	−42.5%	+ 7.5%	+ 7.5%	+ 7.5%
Annualized return	−85.0%	+15.0%	+15.0%	+15.0%

*100 shares at $20, yielding $.10 quarterly
†six-month option at $6, having a $15 exercise price

Table 3. Selling deep in-the-money covered call options

	Prices in Six Months			
Stock*	$ 5	$ 10	$ 20	$ 40
Call†	0	0	10	30
Profit or (loss) on stock	(1500)	(1000)	0	2000
Profit or (loss) on call	1050	1050	50	(1950)
Dividends received	20	20	20	20
T-bill interest on $1050	50	50	50	50
Total profit or (loss)	(380)	120	120	120
Six-month return on $2,000 investment	−19.0%	+ 6.0%	+ 6.0%	+ 6.0%
Annualized return	−38.0%	+12.0%	+12.0%	+12.0%

*100 shares at $20, yielding $.10 quarterly
†six-month option at $10.50, having a $10 exercise price

likely to be offset by an occasional large loser. Selling normally valued, in-the-money calls is superior to shorting against the box, yet I would not call it hedging, since we are dealing with fairly-valued instruments on both sides of the position. It is a tactic useful only to those seeking tax deferral, and possibly to traders who do not want to give up a stock position. As an ongoing investment strategy, brokerage commissions alone will likely exceed any expected incremental returns above risk-free money market rates.

The examples demonstrate how "hedging" normally valued securities cannot be expected to produce high, risk-adjusted rates of return. However, it is surprising how many investors use such strategies, especially the popular selling of call options against their common stock holdings, without knowledge of the potential risks.

HEDGING OVERPRICED SECURITIES

When listed call options first began trading in 1973, most were overpriced. These pricing aberrations lasted for about three years until banks, insurance companies, mutual funds, and other large pools of money moved into the

Table 4. Selling overpriced covered call options

	Prices in Six Months			
Stock*	$ 5	$ 15	$ 20	$ 40
Call†	0	0	5	25
Profit or (loss) on stock	(1500)	(500)	0	2000
Profit or (loss) on call	700	700	200	(1800)
Dividends received	20	20	20	20
T-bill interest on $700	35	35	35	35
Total profit or (loss)	(745)	255	255	255
Six-month return on $2,000 investment	−37.25%	+12.75%	+12.75%	+12.75%
Annualized return	−74.5%	+25.5%	+25.5%	+25.5%

*100 shares at $20, yielding $.10 quarterly
†six-month option at $7, having a $15 exercise price

strategy. As a result of increased selling pressure, premium levels drifted downward to the point that most call options were no longer overvalued. However, overpriced calls can still be found from time to time.

Table 4 illustrates the sale of an overpriced call option. For comparison purposes, I have again assumed an in-the-money call having a $15 exercise price with the underlying common stock trading at $20. Instead of the $6 call premium previously used, I have increased the premium to $7. The extra $100 for six months equals an additional 5.25 percent on the $2,000 investment, or 10.5 percent annualized (10 percent for the higher option premium plus 0.5 percent for extra interest earned). In this example, the covered writing *hedge* provides an annualized return of 25.5 percent at all future stock prices above $15, compared to the 15-percent return when selling a normally valued $6 call.

Writing overpriced calls can be a winning strategy, but are such attractive opportunities available in today's market? The answer is a qualified yes. There are, on occasion, pockets of pricing inefficiencies available to individual investors simply because the professional option writers are not interested in taking small positions, or they have a negative opinion of the underlying common stock. However, be aware that if such an overpriced option is found, the high retail commission expenses to buy the stock, sell the call, and later close out the position when the option expires, will likely eradicate any amount of overvaluation. (Finding an overpriced replacement in the same company when the original call expires would be highly unlikely, thus forcing sale of the underlying common and incurring commissions for both in and out transactions.)

Another word of caution is in order: The $7 call price, may, in fact, be a fair value based on the market's perception of *future* stock-price volatility. If the stock had recently run up from $10 to $20 based on an anticipated takeover at $25 per share, for instance, the covered writing position involves above-average risk if the takeover falls through. In this event the stock could suddenly fall back to $10, leaving covered call writers with large losses. The high option premium might, therefore, properly reflect the risks involved.

While I am trying to discourage you from blindly jumping into the options game, I recognize that it's a popular "sport" that cannot be dismissed lightly; it requires in-depth analysis simply because so many investors are involved. Therefore, Chapters 1 and 2 are devoted exclusively to listed stock option strategies, with special attention given to covered writing.

Although, as you will see, most option strategies should be avoided by serious investors, normally valued calls *can* be important risk-reduction tools when protecting *undervalued* securities on the long side of the hedge. Let's examine the purchase of an undervalued convertible bond, hedged by both the normally- and overvalued call options from the previous examples.

HEDGING UNDERVALUED SECURITIES

The convertible securities market provides the basis for profitable hedging strategies. Of the approximately 1,000 different convertible bonds, convertible preferred stocks, and warrants, there are always pockets of pricing inefficiencies that can be exploited by noninstitutional-sized investors. Undervalued convertible bonds (Chapters 4 and 5) have outperformed the higher-risk stock market averages, an accomplishment few professional money managers using common stocks have attained. These convertibles are well-suited for the risk-reducing hedging strategies discussed in Chapters 6 through 10.

As a preview, let's compare the sale of covered calls against an undervalued convertible bond with the covered writing examples using common stock that you just studied. Exhibit 1 provides risk-reward calculations for a 6-percent bond having a conversion ratio of 50 shares and trading at 102 ($1,020), with an underlying common-stock value of $20. Since the bond's conversion value is 100 (50 shares × $20 per share = $1,000), it is trading at a modest conversion

Exhibit 1. Selling normally-valued call options against undervalued convertibles

		Prices in Six Months		
Stock*	$ 5	$ 15	$ 20	$ 40
Convertible†	60	85	102	200
Call‡	0	0	5	25
Profit or (loss) on convertibles	(840)	(340)	0	1960
Profit or (loss) on call	600	600	100	(1900)
Convertible bond interest received	60	60	60	60
T-bill interest on $600	30	30	30	30
Total profit or (loss)	(150)	350	190	150
Six-month return on $2,040 investment	− 7.4%	+17.2%	+ 9.3%	+ 7.4%
Annualized return	−14.8%	+34.4%	+18.6%	+14.8%

*stock = $20
†two 6% bonds that convert into 50 shares each (100 shares total), trading at 102 ($1,020 each)
‡six-month option at $6, having a $15 exercise price

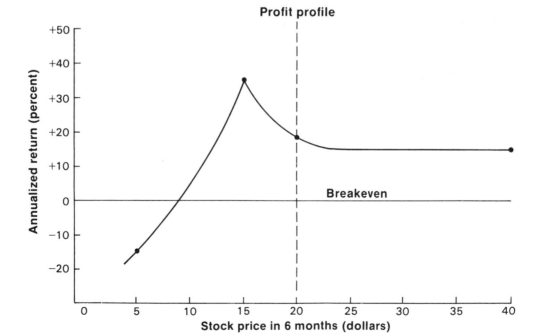

premium of only 2 percent ($1,020 ÷ $1,000 = 1.02). The bond is obviously underpriced relative to the common; it offers the upside potential of the stock, higher income, and much less risk should the stock decline.

The risk-reward calculations of Exhibit 1 are based on the normally-valued $6 call premium. As shown by the calculations and accompanying profit profile, the convertible bond/call-option hedge is expected to produce a profit at all future stock prices above $9 per share, its downside break-even point. The maximum annualized return of 34 percent occurs at the option's $15 strike price, at which point the bond (at 85) would be trading at a 13-percent conversion premium. At higher prices, the profit potential drifts off to a 15-percent annualized return as the bonds loses its premium over conversion value. Compared to the stock/call-option position of Table 2, the convertible hedge offers the same upside potential along with greater downside safety—the key to successful long-term investing. The sale of normally valued call options against undervalued convertible bonds can be a winning investment strategy, even after brokerage commissions.

HEDGING UNDERVALUED SECURITIES
WITH OVERPRICED CALL OPTIONS

A nearly perfect investment strategy occurs when an overpriced call option is available for selling against an undervalued convertible bond. This desirable combination is illustrated by the risk-reward calculations and profit profile of Exhibit 2, using the overpriced $15 call option trading at $7. The extra $100 premium for six months provides an additional 10.3-percent annualized rate of return, or reduced risk, at all future stock prices. A probability analysis would indicate an expected return of more than twice that of risk-free money-market instruments.

Unfortunately, it is difficult to find such attractive opportunities in today's market. There are too many financial sharpshooters waiting for situations like this to come along. The example, however, will help pave the way for advanced SuperHedging strategies you will learn about later—profitable, low-risk strategies that I expect will be available to noninstitutional-sized investors for years to come. Among a variety of sophisticated tactics, you will learn how to find and use overpriced call options effectively in combination with portfolios of under-valued convertible bonds.

Exhibit 2. Selling overpriced call options against undervalued convertibles

	Prices in Six Months			
Stock*	$ 5	$ 15	$ 20	$ 40
Convertible†	60	85	102	200
Call‡	0	0	5	25
Profit or (loss) on convertibles	(840)	(340)	0	1960
Profit or (loss) on call	700	700	200	(1800)
Convertible bond interest received	60	60	60	60
T-bill interest on $700	35	35	35	35
Total profit or (loss)	(45)	455	295	255
Six-month return on $2,040 investment	− 2.2%	+22.3%	+14.5%	+12.5%
Annualized return	− 4.4%	+44.6%	+29.0%	+25.0%

*stock = $20
†two 6% bonds that convert into 50 shares each (100 shares total), trading at 102 ($1,020 each)
‡six-month option at $7, having a $15 exercise price

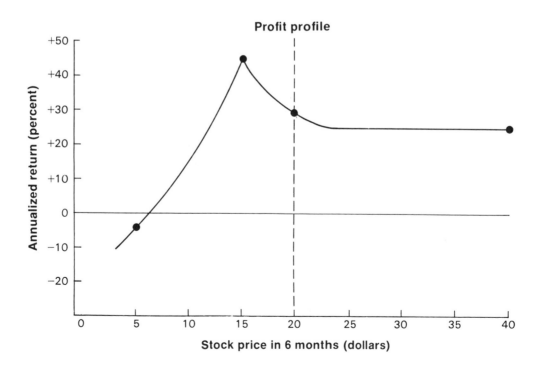

Profit profile

WHY HEDGE?

Over the past sixty years, high-quality common stocks have provided total returns (dividends plus capital appreciation) of about 9.5 percent annually, compared with returns of about 3.2 percent for risk-free U.S. government Treasury bills and 3.0 percent for inflation. Over the ten years ending in 1984, with inflation averaging nearly 8 percent, stocks and T-bills have maintained their historical relationships by returning about 15 and 9 percent, respectively.

The risk-reward relationships for common stocks and risk-free money market instruments are illustrated by the capital market line in Exhibit 3. The horizontal axis indicates relative risks, whereas the vertical axis shows expected returns.

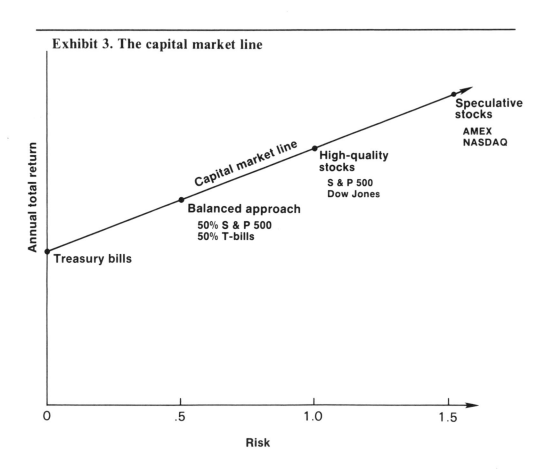

Exhibit 3. The capital market line

By definition, a portfolio of high-quality common stocks represents average risk; U.S. government Treasury bills are risk-free.

As one can conclude by analysis of historical data, common stocks have been the only financial instruments that have enabled investors to build real wealth. However, most investors, remembering either the great stock-market crash of the 1930s, or the more recent bear market of 1973–74, are naturally reluctant to place a large portion of their capital in the stock market. Most, therefore, own some stocks but search out safer havens for the bulk of their investment capital. They are thus prevented from building real wealth, since inflation and taxes steadily erode the purchasing power of their hard-earned savings.

Exhibit 4. Convertible hedging strategies versus the capital market line.

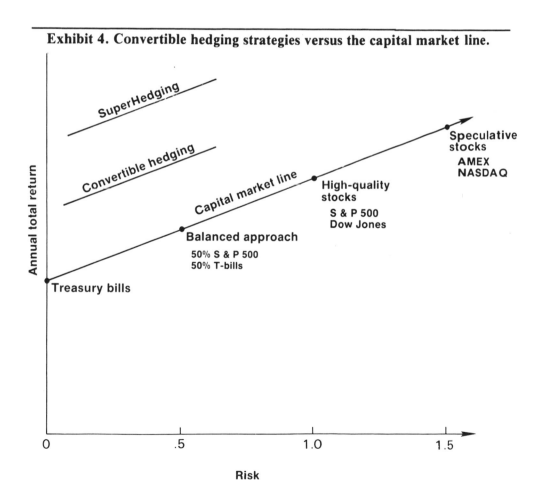

Low-risk convertible hedging strategies are the answer for these conservative investors. Carefully-selected convertibles, hedged by the sale of call options or other financial instruments, can provide the long-term appreciation of the stock market at a risk level below that of balanced portfolios containing stocks and money market instruments. Thus, informed investors can earn high returns on their *total portfolios* without incurring the risk of common stock ownership. The risks and rewards for convertible hedging strategies are compared to the capital market line in Exhibit 4. As shown, these sophisticated strategies offer higher returns than traditional investing, at less risk.

Let's now begin our journey through the fascinating and profitable world of convertible hedging. Section I will challenge conventional wisdom as well as provide the tools necessary for mastering the advanced strategies to be presented later. Section II covers traditional convertible bond hedging tactics; the book concludes with Section III's new SuperHedging strategies.

BASIC STRATEGIES WITH LISTED OPTIONS

CHAPTER 1

Basic Put and Call Option Strategies

Listed put and call options can be important tools for reducing a portfolio's risk. However, although these financial instruments were introduced by the Chicago Board Options Exchange (CBOE) in 1973, the investing public is still largely unaware of—or misinformed about—their capabilities. Even skilled option specialists recognize the need to reevaluate their tactics from time to time. The Deficit Reduction Act of 1984, for example, drastically altered the way puts, calls, and related stock positions are treated for tax purposes. Since the passage of the Deficit Reduction Act some strategies are no longer appropriate for tax-paying investors, whereas others have become more attractive.

Option trading by inexperienced investors enhances commission revenues to the brokerage community and increases profits to marketmakers trading for their own accounts. High commissions costs from frequent turnover, plus forfeiture of the bid-ask price spread via carelessly entered at-the-market orders to buy or sell, can only produce poor results. Therefore, it is important to master the basic option strategies and their relationship to conventional investing in common stocks and money-market instruments before considering any involvement in the option markets. This background is essential, both to avoid costly pitfalls and to utilize the more advanced (and more profitable) hedging strategies I will present in later chapters.

In the examples that follow, as well as in others throughout the book, I exclude brokerage commissions for ease of illustration. Some strategies involve few commission dollars, whereas others are quite costly, depending on such factors as portfolio turnover, order size, and your stockbroker's commission schedule. You should always include commissions in your risk-reward calculations, because any high-commission option strategy is doomed to failure. I do not make this statement lightly—*there are no exceptions!*

Since the various strategies may be used both by individual investors and by tax-exempt trusts, taxes are also excluded from the risk-reward calculations. Tax-paying investors, however, should always strive for maximum after-tax returns; they should select only those strategies offering potential for long-term capital gains.

Under current tax law, securities held for more than six months are treated as long-term capital gains or losses. While I do not recommend frequent *stock* trading for tax purposes (brokerage commissions will likely offset any tax advantages gained), certain *option* strategies are well-suited for optimizing after-tax returns. Most strategies involving the *purchase* of puts or calls by tax-paying investors should limit selections to those having a life exceeding six months. As the six-month holding period nears, losers may be sold for short-term losses; winners should be held at least six months and one day for long-term capital gains. Note that, like the short sale of common stock, gains or losses on puts and calls *sold* are short-term regardless of the holding period.

Bear in mind, however, that the Deficit Reduction Act of 1984, an exceedingly complex and far-reaching piece of legislation, affects investors employing options in *offsetting positions.* For example, earlier legislation decreed that the purchase of a put option, when holding the underlying common stock, was an offsetting position, and therefore terminated the stock's holding period; the 1984 Act stated that the sale of a deep in-the-money call option also terminates the stock's holding period.

The concept of offsetting positions embodies a *substantial reduction of risk* test. To what extent this vaguely-worded legislation will be applied to the innumerable tactics available in the financial markets has yet to be determined by the Internal Revenue Service. Until the IRS issues regulations clarifying the Act's provisions, uncertainties will remain. Thus, any discussion of tax consequences for the strategies presented throughout this book should be confirmed by expert tax counsel. (See Appendix A for possible IRS rulings on various option strategies.

BASIC OPTION STRATEGIES

There are seven basic investment strategies involving puts and calls: three are bullish, three are bearish, and the neutral seventh is a direct alternative to money market instruments. Each of the seven strategies (listed below) involves the purchase or short sale of common stock (1, 2, ...), while its alternative (1a, 2a, ...) excludes the use of stock. Thus, each basic strategy offers two choices. In some cases the choice between the stock strategy and its alternative will be a toss-up; in other cases the risk-reward calculations, brokerage commissions, and income tax consequences will favor one over the other. My examples will indicate the best choice for both tax-exempt trusts and tax-paying individuals.

For the purpose of this discussion, I will assume that the most bullish market strategy is the ownership of common stock (Strategy 1); the most bearish is the short sale (Strategy 7). Options may be employed by themselves or in combination with stocks when constructing alternatives to these extremes, or for any risk-reward posture in between. Listed in order of the most bullish to the most bearish, the seven basic strategies are as follows:

Bullish strategies

1. Buy 100 shares of stock.
1a. Buy one call and sell one put.

2. Buy 100 shares of stock and buy one put.
2a. Buy one call.

3. Buy 100 shares of stock and sell one call.
3a. Sell one put.

Neutral strategies

4. Buy 100 shares of stock, buy one put, and sell one call.
4a. Buy Treasury bills.

Bearish strategies

5. Short 100 shares of stock and sell one put.
5a. Sell one call.

   6.   Short 100 shares of stock and buy one call.
   6a. Buy one put.

   7.   Short 100 shares of stock.
   7a. Buy one put and sell one call.

All other option tactics, such as straddles and spreads, may be analyzed by combining two or more of the basic strategies. The popular straddle sales and purchases are presented later as strategies 8a and 9a.

   Before selecting a particular strategy, investors should construct a risk-reward analysis table and profit profile graph similar to the examples I have prepared in the following pages. These basic tools, unused by most nonprofessional investors, identify a strategy's risk and profit potential. Unfortunately, most investors who have lost money in "conservative" option strategies and wondered why were simply unaware of the risks they unknowingly assumed. Successful investing *demands* a thorough understanding of the risks involved.

   The risk-reward calculations in the examples are based on certain assumptions that simplify the arithmetic.

- The common stock is trading at $20.
- The common stock pays a $.10 quarterly dividend (2 percent annual yield).
- A six-month call option, having an exercise (strike) price of $20, is trading at $2 ($200 for each at-the-money call on 100 shares of stock).
- A six-month put option, also having a $20 strike price, is trading at $1.25 ($125 for each at-the-money put on 100 shares of stock).
- Each position, an investment of $2,000 based on 100 shares, is held until the options expire in six months.
- Options are assumed to be trading at their intrinsic values at expiration.
- Unused funds, or premiums received from option sales, are placed in U.S. Treasury bills (or other risk-free money market instruments) yielding 10 percent.

   Each strategy is evaluated by a risk-reward analysis for stock prices of $10, $20, $30, and $40 six months later at the option's expiration. A profit profile, which graphically shows gains and losses for any future stock price over the $10 to $40 range, follows each risk-reward calculation table. I chose the $10 and $40 extremes for analysis purposes simply because they encompass a broad price range; and, while most stocks will not move this far in six months, a stock's halving and doubling are roughly equal probabilities.

Let's now evaluate the risk-reward characteristics plus the pros and cons for each of the stragegies (Exhibits 1-1 through 1-9). Study the examples carefully. They are not complex if you take a few minutes to become comfortable with them. To check your comprehension after you have finished the chapter, go back and look only at the profit profiles. You should be able to identify the strategies without reference to the risk-reward calculation tables or text.

EXHIBIT 1–1. BULLISH STRATEGIES 1 AND 1a

Investment Objective: To achieve long-term capital appreciation in a rising stock market.

Strategy 1 is the conventional purchase of common stock—100 shares at $20 each for a $2,000 investment. Paying only a 2-percent annual dividend, most appreciation will be taxed as long-term capital gains if held longer than six months. The profit profile is a straight line showing a $980 six-month loss at a future price of $10, and a $2,020 gain at $40.

Alternative Strategy 1a fabricates a common stock position through the simultaneous purchase of a call option and the sale of a put, both trading at-the-money. The net cost to execute this option alternative is only $75—$125 received from the put sale minus $200 paid for the call. The $1,925 balance of the $2,000 investment is placed in Treasury bills earning 10 percent, or about $95 for six months (all figures will be rounded to the nearest $5). The option strategy is also expected to lose $980 at a future stock price of $10 and gain $2,020 at $40; its straight-line profit profile is identical to that of Strategy 1.

Commissions: When trading in unit sizes above one put and one call, the total commissions for both options are usually less than those for common stock. However, with a possible exception for very active traders, commissions will likely be less for stock ownership over the long run, since it avoids the added expense of rolling options over every six months.

Taxes: Income taxes also favor common stock ownership, since most of the return from a T-bill/option program will likely be fully-taxable interest income instead of capital gains. Also, pending clarification of the substantial reduction of risk test, it may not be possible to achieve long-term gains on profitable calls when a put option is sold short in combination with the call.

Preferred Strategy

- Tax-exempt investors: Strategy 1
- High-tax-bracket investors: Strategy 1

Exhibit 1-1. Bullish strategies 1 and 1a

	Price	*Prices at Expiration (6 months)*			
Stock	$ 20.00	$ 10	20	$ 30	$ 40
Call	2.00	0	0	10	20
Put	1.25	10	0	0	0

Strategy 1: Buy 100 shares of stock

Profit or (loss) on stock	(1000)	0	1000	2000
Dividends received	20	20	20	20
Total profit or (loss)	(980)	20	1020	2020

Strategy 1a: Buy one call and sell one put

Profit or (loss) on call	(200)	(200)	800	1800
Profit or (loss) on put	(875)	125	125	125
T-bill interest on $1,925	95	95	95	95
Total profit or (loss)	(980)	20	1020	2020

Profit profile (strategies 1 and 1a)

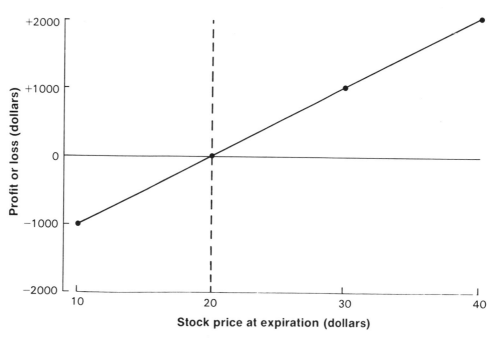

EXHIBIT 1–2. BULLISH STRATEGIES 2 AND 2a

Investment Objective: To achieve most of the upside potential of common stock ownership while limiting downside risk.

Strategy 2 involves the purchase of common stock in combination with a "protective put." Puts are often recommended by stockbrokers as insurance against a stock-price decline; however, the strategy reduces upside profits by the premium paid to acquire the put ($125 per 100 shares), and the value of money to carry it ($5). The strategy's most serious drawback, seldom mentioned by those suggesting it, is its loss in a static market in which the stock's price does not change materially. The profit profile illustrates these risk-reward characteristics.

Alternative Strategy 2a is the purchase of a call option for $200 with the $1,800 balance placed in Treasury bills. Its risk-reward calculations and profit profile are the same as for Strategy 2—a maximum risk of $125 and an $1,890 total return if the stock doubles to $40.

Commissions: While the purchase of the cheaper put option can mean slightly lower commissions than the purchase of the higher-priced call, any turnover of the stock position in Strategy 2 will likely result in higher commission expenses, over the long run, than those incurred with Strategy 2a.

Taxes: Since a put purchase terminates the stock's holding period under current tax law, it is difficult to protect a stock portfolio with put options and achieve long-term capital gains. There is an exception, called a "married put," but this tactic will likely generate excessive commissions. The call option purchase of Strategy 2a is relatively straightforward. Thus, any profits above T-bill earnings should be taxable at the lower rates for long-term gains if the call option portfolio is carefully managed; losers should be sold prior to the six-month holding period and winners held for more than six months.

Preferred Strategy

- Tax-exempt investors: Strategy 2a
- High-tax-bracket investors: Strategy 2a

Exhibit 1-2. Bullish strategies 2 and 2a

	Price	*Prices at Expiration (6 months)*			
		$ 10	$ 20	$ 30	$ 40
Stock	$ 20.00	$ 10	$ 20	$ 30	$ 40
Call	2.00	0	0	10	20
Put	1.25	10	0	0	0

Strategy 2: Buy 100 shares of stock and buy one put

Profit or (loss) on stock	(1000)	0	1000	2000
Profit or (loss) on put	875	(125)	(125)	(125)
Interest charge on $125	(5)	(5)	(5)	(5)
Dividends received	20	20	20	20
Total profit or (loss)	(110)	(110)	890	1890

Strategy 2a: Buy one call

Profit or (loss) on call	(200)	(200)	800	1800
T-bill interest on $1,800	90	90	90	90
Total profit or (loss)	(110)	(110)	890	1890

Profit profile (strategies 2 and 2a)

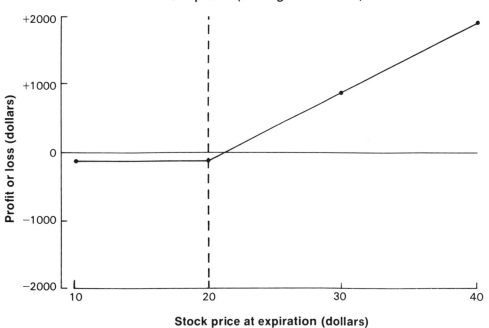

EXHIBIT 1–3. BULLISH STRATEGIES 3 AND 3a

Investment Objective: Although widely touted as a means to earn "extra income" from one's portfolio, the correct investment objective for these strategies is simply to achieve a modest return in a static or rising stock market.

Strategy 3 is the ever-popular sale of covered calls. As shown by the risk-reward calculations and profit profile, the premium received provides an above-average return in a static market, $230 for six months. While covered-call writing does reduce downside losses by the amount of the premium, losses can be substantial—$770 if the stock drops to $10, for example. Another disadvantage occurs in a rising market, when losses on the calls offset most of the common stock's gain, thereby capping profits at only $230 regardless of how high the stock might rise. Chapter 2 will analyze this strategy in greater detail, since it is widely used by individuals and professional money managers alike.

Alternative Strategy 3a is the less-popular, but simpler, sale of put options against Treasury bills. Also promoted as a way to earn "extra income," or as a chance to purchase stocks at prices below their current markets when the strategy fails to work, the T-bill/put-option strategy will produce only short-term capital gains and fully taxable income.

Commissions: The commissions generated from selling covered calls will often be much higher than the alternative sale of put options against Treasury bills. However, careful portfolio management can keep commissions down to a reasonable level.

Taxes: The covered-call-writing strategy can be managed to provide mostly long-term capital gains compared to taxable income and short-term gains for the put-option alternative.

Preferred Strategy

- Tax-exempt investors: Strategy 3a
- High-tax-bracket investors: Strategy 3 (assuming nominal commissions)

Exhibit 1-3. Bullish strategies 3 and 3a

	Price	Prices at Expiration (6 months)			
Stock	$ 20.00	$ 10	$ 20	$ 30	$ 40
Call	2.00	0	0	10	20
Put	1.25	10	0	0	0

Strategy 3: Buy 100 shares of stock and sell one call

Profit or (loss) on stock	(1000)	0	1000	2000
Profit or (loss) on call	200	200	(800)	(1800)
T-bill interest on $200	10	10	10	10
Dividends received	20	20	20	20
Total profit or (loss)	(770)	230	230	230

Strategy 3a: Sell one put

Profit or (loss) on put	(875)	125	125	125
T-bill interest on $2,125	105	105	105	105
Total profit or (loss)	(770)	230	230	230

Profit profile (strategies 3 and 3a)

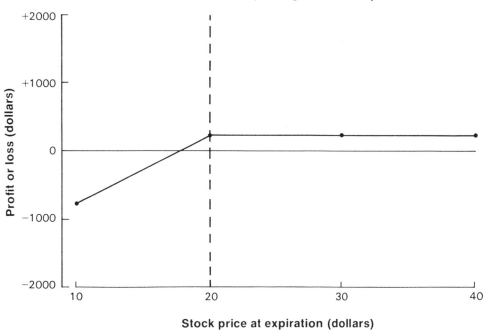

EXHIBIT 1–4. BULLISH STRATEGIES 4 AND 4a

Investment Objective: To achieve a risk-free rate of return equal to or higher than money market instruments.

Strategy 4 is a direct alternative to risk-free money-market instruments. Puts are purchased and calls sold against ownership of common stock. In effect, the put/call combination "fabricates" a short sale of common stock. Unlike the profitless short sale against the box, earning are available from the fabricated short sale tactic—the difference between premiums received from the calls sold and premiums paid for the puts purchased, in addition to dividends.

This strategy is termed a "conversion" and is widely used by brokerage firms and the option marketmakers when investing their own capital. However, conversions are not a viable strategy for the commission-paying public investor who is unable to access and take advantage of temporary pricing aberrations. However, the strategy can be used effectively by those already invested in the bullish option-hedging programs of Strategies 2 and 3 who wish to shift to a more conservative stance. Without incurring high commission expenses by disrupting their core stock holdings, stock/put-option hedgers in Strategy 2 can achieve a risk-free posture through the additional sale of calls. Covered-call writers of Strategy 3 can also inexpensively shift to a riskless posture by buying puts.

Strategy 4a is the straightforward purchase of Treasury bills or other short-term money-market instruments. Its profit profile is identical to that of Strategy 4, $100 for six months.

Commissions: Strategy 4 would generate huge commissions, whereas the alternative T-bill purchase involves no commissions.

Taxes: Pending clarification of the substantial reduction of risk test by the IRS, Strategy 4 is likely to produce only short-term capital gains in addition to modest income. However, it might be appropriate for investors with large tax loss carryforwards, provided it could be executed at minimal commission expense.

Preferred Strategy

- Tax-exempt investors: Strategy 4a
- High-tax-bracket investors: Strategy 4a

Exhibit 1-4. Neutral strategies 4 and 4a

	Price	*Prices at Expiration (6 months)*			
Stock	$ 20.00	10	$ 20	$ 30	$ 40
Call	2.00	0	0	10	20
Put	1.25	10	0	0	0

Strategy 4: Buy 100 shares of stock, buy one put, and sell one call

Profit or (loss) on stock	(1000)	0	1000	2000
Profit or (loss) on put	875	(125)	(125)	(125)
Profit or (loss) on call	200	200	(800)	(1800)
T-bill interest on $75	5	5	5	5
Dividends received	20	20	20	20
Total profit or (loss)	100	100	100	100

Strategy 4a: Buy Treasury bills

T-bill interest on $2,000	100	100	100	100

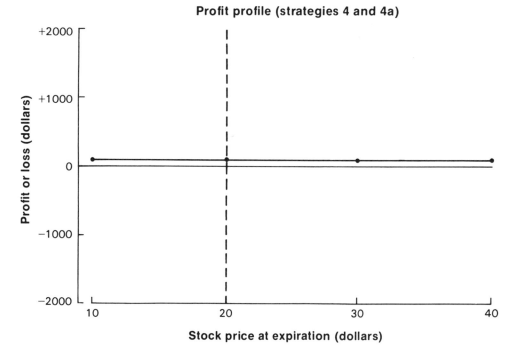

Profit profile (strategies 4 and 4a)

EXHIBIT 1–5. BULLISH STRATEGIES 5 AND 5a

Investment Objective: To achieve a modest return in a static or declining stock market.

Strategy 5 involves the short sale of common stock combined with the sale of a put. As shown by the risk-reward calculations, the put premium reduces upside risk somewhat, but also cancels out most of the short sale's downside profit potential. It's a mirror image of bullish covered-call writing, Strategy 3. Large losses will be experienced if the stock advances, instead of declining as anticipated. Note that the stock short-seller must borrow the shares, and is therefore required to pay the $10 quarterly dividends to the lender.

Alternative Strategy 5a, the sale of a naked call option against Treasury bills or other marginable money market instruments, is far superior; it provides an extra $100 return at all possible outcomes. The reason for its advantage is that, except for certain professionals, short sellers of stock do not get the use of the short-sale proceeds. The strategy, however, will provide a maximum return of only $310 for six months if everything goes as planned. The profit profile is based on the higher returns from Strategy 5a.

Commissions: The commissions generated by the short-stock/short-put program of Strategy 5 will be much higher than those generated by the naked call option alternative.

Taxes: Both strategies involve short positions; therefore, the opportunity to obtain long-term capital gains does not exist. Any capital gains or losses will be short-term regardless of how long the position is held.

Preferred Strategy

- Tax-exempt investors: Strategy 5a
- High-tax-bracket investors: Strategy 5a

Exhibit 1-5. Bearish strategies 5 and 5a

	Price	*Prices at Expiration (6 months)*			
Stock	$ 20.00	$ 10	$ 20	$ 30	$ 40
Call	2.00	0	0	10	20
Put	1.25	10	0	0	0

Strategy 5: Short 100 shares of stock and sell one put

Profit or (loss) on stock	1000	0	(1000)	(2000)
Profit or (loss) on put	(875)	125	125	125
T-bill interest on $2,125	105	105	105	105
Dividends paid	(20)	(20)	(20)	(20)
Total profit or (loss)	210	210	(790)	(1790)

Strategy 5a: Sell one call

Profit or (loss) on call	200	200	(800)	(1800)
T-bill interest on $2,200	110	110	110	110
Total profit or (loss)	310	310	(690)	(1690)

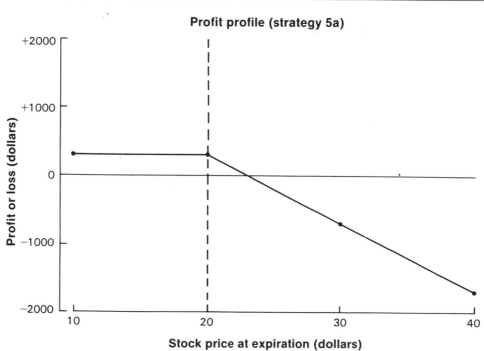

Profit profile (strategy 5a)

EXHIBIT 1–6. BULLISH STRATEGIES 6 AND 6a

Investment Objective: To achieve most of the downside potential of a declining stock price while limiting upside risk.

Strategy 6 is the short sale of common stock in combination with a protective call. The position achieves the full downside potential of a short sale, reduced by the premium paid to acquire the call. It's a mirror image of the ownership of stock and a protective put of bullish Strategy 2.

Alternative Strategy 6a is the more-straightforward purchase of a put option combined with Treasury bills. As with Strategy 5a, this alternative provides an extra $100 return at all possible outcomes. Since most of the put's purchase cost is offset by interest earned on the T-bills, the maximum six-month risk is only $30. The profit profile is based on the higher returns from Strategy 6a.

Commissions: The commissions for purchasing puts in Strategy 6a will be far lower than those for buying both common stock and call options, as in Strategy 6.

Taxes: Any capital gains earned by the stock/call-option strategy of Strategy 6 will be short-term. However, the put option purchase of Strategy 6a is one of the few ways to profit in a declining stock market while achieving long-term capital gains. Unlike the short sale of common stock, which is treated as short-term regardless of how long it is held, a *purchased* put will be long-term if held more than six months. For this reason, in addition to its low-risk characteristics, I view Strategy 6a as the best approach for those who are bearish on the market.

Preferred Strategy

- Tax-exempt investors: Strategy 6a
- High-tax-bracket investors: Strategy 6a

Exhibit 1-6. Bearish strategies 6 and 6a

	Price	*Prices at Expiration (6 months)*			
Stock	$ 20.00	$ 10	$ 20	$ 30	$ 40
Call	2.00	0	0	10	20
Put	1.25	10	0	0	0

Strategy 6: Short 100 shares of stock and buy one call

Profit or (loss) on stock	1000	0	(1000)	(2000)
Profit or (loss) on call	(200)	(200)	800	1800
T-bill interest on $1,800	90	90	90	90
Dividends paid	(20)	(20)	(20)	(20)
Total profit or (loss)	870	(130)	(130)	(130)

Strategy 6a: Buy one put

Profit or (loss) on put	875	(125)	(125)	(125)
T-bill interest on $1,875	95	95	95	95
Total profit or (loss)	970	(30)	(30)	(30)

Profit profile (strategy 6a)

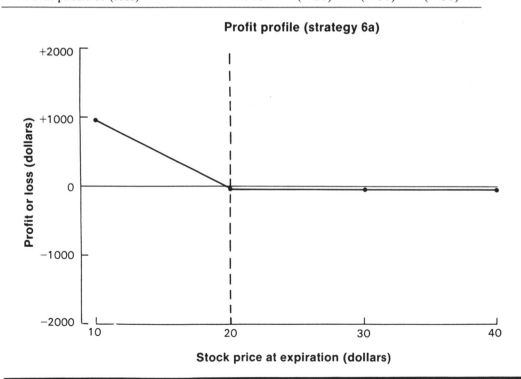

EXHIBIT 1–7. BULLISH STRATEGIES 7 AND 7a

Investment Objective: To achieve a high return in a declining stock market.

Strategy 7 is the highly-speculative short sale of common stock. Profits are earned if the stock declines as anticipated, but losses can be unlimited if the stock advances. Interest is earned on Treasury bills deposited in the account to margin the short sale; any stock dividends must be paid by the short seller to the lender.

Alternative Strategy 7a fabricates a common-stock short sale through the simultaneous purchase of a put option and the sale of a call. As with Strategies 5a and 6a, this option alternative provides an extra $100 return at all possible outcomes. The profit profile is based on the higher returns from Strategy 7a.

Commissions: Commission expenses will favor the put/call-option alternative of Strategy 7a if traded in unit sizes greater than one option each. However, the ongoing commissions for both strategies will likely be quite high, since most short sellers quickly cut their losses if the stock turns against them, resulting in abnormally-high portfolio turnover.

Taxes: The short sale of stock of Strategy 7 will produce only short-term capital gains or losses. Pending clarification of the substantial reduction of risk test, any capital gain from the put/call alternative might also be treated as short-term. This assumes that the call-option sale is determined to be an offsetting position and thus terminates the put's holding period (see Appendix A), an assumption I find hard to accept for the high-risk example illustrated.

Preferred Strategy

- Tax-exempt investors: Strategy 7a
- High-tax-bracket investors: Strategy 7a

Exhibit 1-7. Bearish strategies 7 and 7a

	Price	*Prices at Expiration (6 months)*			
Stock	$ 20.00	$ 10	$ 20	$ 30	$ 40
Call	2.00	0	0	10	20
Put	1.25	10	0	0	0

Strategy 7: Short 100 shares of stock

Profit or (loss) on stock	1000	0	(1000)	(2000)
T-bill interest on $2,000	100	100	100	100
Dividends paid	(20)	(20)	(20)	(20)
Total profit or (loss)	1080	80	(920)	(1920)

Strategy 7a: Buy one put and sell one call

Profit or (loss) on put	875	(125)	(125)	(125)
Profit or (loss) on call	200	200	(800)	(1800)
T-bill interest on $2,075	105	105	105	105
Total profit or (loss)	1180	180	(820)	(1820)

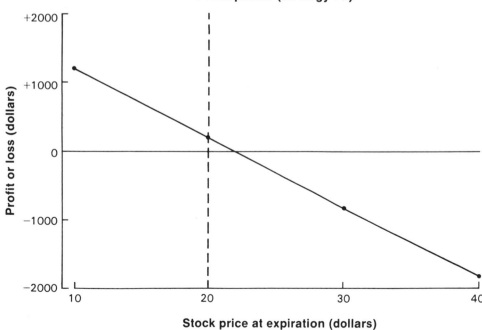

Profit profile (strategy 7a)

EXHIBIT 1–8. BULLISH STRATEGIES 8 AND 8a

Investment Objective: To achieve a high return in a static stock market.

Strategy 8 is a call option-ratio hedge—the sale of more than one call against 100 shares of stock. A 2-to-1 hedge is illustrated and shows a positive return over a price range of about $15.50 to $24.50 on the option's expiration date. If the stock ends up unchanged at $20, the maximum profit of $440 will be earned. This strategy is widely used by professionals when option premiums are *overpriced* and calls are trading out of the money. Its obvious disadvantage is the potential for loss in both rising and declining markets.

In theory, one should be able to close out the position without significant loss if the upper or lower break-even points were reached—the loss would equal the options' remaining time value plus commissions. In practice, however, an unexpected announcement, such as a takeover offer, could result in an immediate price move well past the break-even price. Thus, occasional large losses could wipe out numerous small profits.

Alternative Strategy 8a, known as a straddle, is the simultaneous sale of one put and one call against money-market instruments. Its risk-reward calculations and profit profile are the same as for Strategy 8.

Commissions: Alternative strategy 8a can be executed at lower commissions, since it avoids the additional purchase of common stock.

Taxes: The short sale of puts and calls, as in Strategy 8a, will produce only short-term capital gains or losses, plus fully taxable T-bill income. Careful management of the ratio hedging of Strategy 8 should provide mostly long-term capital gains.

Preferred Strategy

- Tax-exempt investors: Strategy 8a
- High-tax-bracket investors: Strategy 8

Exhibit 1-8. Option strategies 8 and 8a

	Price	Prices at Expiration (6 months)			
Stock	$ 20.00	$ 10	$ 20	$ 30	$ 40
Call	2.00	0	0	10	20
Put	1.25	10	0	0	0

Strategy 8: Buy 100 shares of stock and sell two calls

Profit or (loss) on stock	(1000)	0	1000	2000
Profit or (loss) on calls	400	400	(1600)	(3600)
T-bill interest on $400	20	20	20	20
Dividends received	20	20	20	20
Total profit or (loss)	(560)	440	(560)	(1560)

Strategy 8a: Sell one put and sell one call

Profit or (loss) on put	(875)	125	125	125
Profit or (loss) on call	200	200	(800)	(1800)
T-bill interest on $2,325	115	115	115	115
Total profit or (loss)	(560)	440	(560)	(1560)

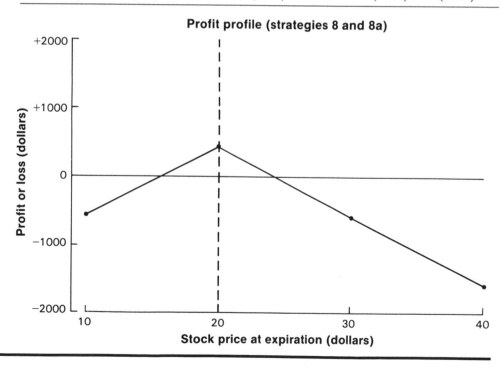

Profit profile (strategies 8 and 8a)

EXHIBIT 1–9. BULLISH STRATEGIES 9 AND 9a

Investment Objective: To achieve a high return in a volatile stock market.

Strategy 9, the purchase of stock combined with the purchase of two puts, is the opposite of Strategy 8; it is designed to profit from a major stock-price move either up or down. A loss will be experienced only if the stock ends up near the exercise price. It is a strategy used by professionals when they expect high future price volatility and put premiums are *undervalued.*

Alternative Strategy 9a, the purchase of a put/call straddle, is a less-costly approach, since it avoids the extra commissions associated with the common stock. Its risk-reward calculations and profit profile are the same as for Strategy 9.

Commissions: Alternative Strategy 9a can be executed at lower commissions.

Taxes: Pending clarification of the substantial reduction of risk test, capital gains from both strategies might be treated as short term. This assumes that the holding period in Strategy 9a is terminated when one holds both a put and a call long (see Appendix A); this is an assumption I find hard to accept for the example illustrated.

One way to avoid any tax complications would be to own puts and calls on different companies. This approach also allows one to purchase the most undervalued puts and calls available and to take maximum advantage of fundamental and/or technical analysis of the underlying common stocks (i.e., to buy undervalued puts on stocks expected to underperform the market and undervalued calls on stocks expected to outperform the market). This tactic would be especially attractive for those who receive short-term gains from other investments—losers would be sold before six months for short-term losses and winners held for long-term gains.

Preferred Strategy

- Tax-exempt investors: Strategy 9a
- High-tax-bracket investors: Strategy 9a

Exhibit 1-9. Option strategies 9 and 9a

	Price	*Prices at Expiration (6 months)*			
		$ 10	$ 20	$ 30	$ 40
Stock	$ 20.00	$ 10	$ 20	$ 30	$ 40
Call	2.00	0	0	10	20
Put	1.25	10	0	0	0

Strategy 9: Buy 100 shares of stock and buy two puts

Profit or (loss) on stock	(1000)	0	1000	2000
Profit or (loss) on puts	1750	(250)	(250)	(250)
Interest charge on $250	(10)	(10)	(10)	(10)
Dividends received	20	20	20	20
Total profit or (loss)	760	(240)	760	1760

Strategy 9a: Buy one put and buy one call

Profit or (loss) on put	875	(125)	(125)	(125)
Profit or (loss) on call	(200)	(200)	800	1800
T-bill interest on $1,675	85	85	85	85
Total profit or (loss)	760	(240)	760	1760

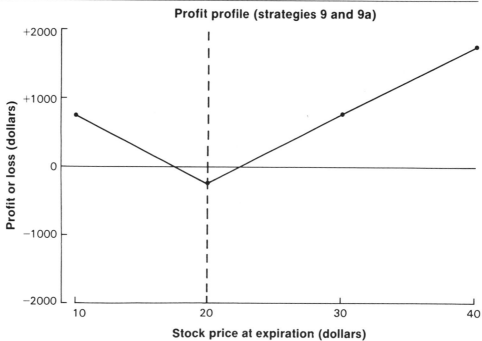

Profit profile (strategies 9 and 9a)

SPREADING OPTIONS

Highly touted by some advisory services and stockbrokers as a "low-risk" way to play the market, there is one option strategy that should *always be avoided by nonprofessional investors.* It is termed "spreading," the simultaneous purchase and sale of puts or calls having different exercise prices or expiration dates. Variations of this term have alluring names, such as "calendar spreads," "bull spreads," "bear spreads," and "butterfly spreads," among others; however, all are virtually guaranteed to destroy one's wealth.

It would take several chapters to illustrate all spreading combinations. In fact, entire books have been devoted to the subject. Suffice it to say that professional marketmakers are the only ones who can execute these strategies profitably. Minimal commissions and constant access to pricing inefficiences are their exclusive advantages. Marketmakers are quick to react to under- or overpriced opportunities by taking the other side of the trade. They then protect their positions with another option that has a different strike price or expiration month. As prices return to normal, often within minutes, they plan to unwind the spread at a profit. In no way can public investors compete against these highly-skilled specialists.

Note that since many options are not actively traded, closing prices often do not reflect the true markets. Investors scanning the financial section of their morning newspapers are usually disappointed when they attempt to execute orders for perceived bargains based on the previous day's close.

This is my advice to those who cannot resist the temptation to trade option spreads: Purchase a seat on an options exchange, roll up your sleeves, and go to work. You will quickly learn that making money by trading options is a full-time, demanding business. Even many of the professional marketmakers find it hard to survive in this competitive environment.

Options can, however, play an important role in portfolio management, but investors who wish to employ them must be selective in their use. I will illustrate the best option strategies in later chapters, but first let's go back to the covered-call writing of Strategy 3, a popular tactic widely employed by both unskilled and professional investors seeking current income.

CHAPTER 2

Writing Covered Call Options

The ever-popular sale of call options against stocks in one's portfolio—covered call writing—is usually described as a conservative strategy that can provide additional income and reduce the risk of stock ownership. Except for the misuse of the term *income* for marketing purposes (profits or losses are capital gains or losses, not income), it is hard to fault the above description. Call-option writing can provide modestly higher returns than stock ownership in a static market, and it does reduce risk. Why, then, have so many covered writers become disillusioned with the strategy? How has it failed to live up to expectations as an investment panacea for participants seeking high current income?

Covered writing is not the simplistic, beat-the-market tactic many investors are led to believe it can be. As with any hedging strategy involving related securities, successful application demands careful analysis of probabilities, in tandem with painstaking portfolio management, to control trading expenses. It is not unusual, for example, to find covered writers paying brokerage commissions equal to the strategy's entire expected return, leaving them monetarily back where they began.

The tradeoff to covered writing for its risk reduction in declining markets is seldom articulated by those promoting this strategy: opportunity loss in rising markets. In addition, as illustrated by Strategy 3 of Chapter 1, covered writing does involve risk. Losses experienced by many unsuspecting covered writers in declining markets have far exceeded the risk they thought they were assuming.

Since the sale of call options is an important risk-reduction tool for the advanced hedging strategies you will learn about later, let's take a closer look at covered writing.

EVALUATING CALL-OPTION PREMIUMS

The only reason to have a covered-writing portfolio is to achieve a higher risk-adjusted rate of return than is available anywhere else. Risk reduction, by itself, is an insufficient reason for an option sale; a comparable low-risk posture can be achieved by simply maintaining a portion of one's portfolio in the money market. Any covered-writing program should be viewed as an alternative to some combination of stocks and money-market instruments. The appropriate stock/money-market mix, for comparison purposes, is related to the risk-reward characteristics of both the options sold and their underlying common stocks—some covered-writing programs are conservative while others are aggressive.

Assuming that the stock and options markets are reasonably efficient, as I believe they are, most covered-writing programs are destined to underperform over the long run. This is virtually guaranteed by the brokerage commissions and any forfeiture of the bid-ask price spread. To come out ahead, you must confine sales to the occasional overpriced situations. Before embarking on an option writing program, you should study the factors that influence option premiums, to learn how to identify the best writing candidates.

The Exercise Price.   All listed options offer at least two different exercise prices. In-the-money calls trade at higher premiums than out-of-the-money calls, thus providing greater downside protection for covered writers, but less profit opportunity.

Time to Expiration. All listed options offer three different expiration dates, ranging up to nine months. Longer-term calls provide the most protection and the least portfolio turnover. Shorter-term calls are usually more liquid, resulting in tighter bid-ask prices.

Interest Rates. Option premiums tend to rise or fall with short-term money market rates. Option sellers, viewing covered writing as an alternative to a combination of stocks and money market instruments, demand higher premiums as interest rates rise. Option buyers are willing to pay these higher premiums because they are earning more on their cash reserves (Strategy 2a of Chapter 1).

Stock Yield. Option premiums are lower on high-dividend stocks; sellers are willing to accept less because the high total return they seek includes the dividends. Similarly, buyers insist on lower premiums since high-yielding stocks usually offer less price-appreciation potential. Table 2-1 summarizes current yields for stocks with listed options in late 1984. Note that the yields on most optionable stocks are well below the S&P 500's 4.7 percent.

Stock Price Volatility. Option premiums are higher on stocks exhibiting greater price volatility. Sellers demand the higher premiums as compensation for the extra risk; buyers are willing to pay more for the increased possibility of large gains. Table 2-2 summarizes five-year relative volatility (RV) data for the stocks with listed options in 1984. Note that whereas an average stock has a 100 RV, the stock market's volatility, as represented by the S&P 500 Index, was only 40. Most individually owned stock portfolios will experience much greater risk than a market index, due to inadequate diversification.

While historical price volatility is useful, the market's perception of future volatility is what really influences premiums. A previously dull stock, for instance, could quickly command high-option premiums if it became a takeover target.

Market Sentiment. Premiums tend to rise in advancing markets. The demand by market speculators increases, and some option sellers may retreat from their normal writing activities, hoping to achieve larger profits. Thus, market sentiment can alter normal supply/demand relationships, creating under- or overpriced opportunities.

Table 2-1. Dividend payments for stocks with listed options

Yield range—%	Number of stocks
0 — 0.9	66
1.0 — 1.9	49
2.0 — 2.9	46
3.0 — 3.9	70
4.0 — 4.9	43
5.0 — 5.9	43
6.0 — 6.9	18
7.0 — 7.9	8
8.0 — 8.9	12
9.0 — 9.9	6
10.0 or more	5
Total stocks	366

Note: Standard & Poor's 500 Stock Index yield = 4.7%
Source: *Value Line Options,* November 26, 1984.

The above variables may be analyzed mathematically to estimate an option's fair market value. Computer software programs are available, as are investment advisory services, to accomplish this task. Those contemplating an option-writing program should avail themselves of one or more of these services. Routine acceptance of the current market price, a practice followed by most nonprofessional writers, will guarantee failure of any option-writing strategy.

CALL OPTION PRICE CURVES

From the 366 different stocks with listed options in November 1984, I chose three for analysis: Boeing, Commonwealth Edison, and Datapoint. Each stock had options on the Feb–May–Aug–Nov cycle; thus, in November, calls were available with three-, six-, and nine-month expirations. In addition, the three stocks, ranging from a staid electric utility to a volatile high-tech company, offered widely different yields and widely different risk-reward characteristics. Table 2-3 presents normal premium data for the three companies, courtesy of *Value Line Options.*

Using the normal option premiums estimated in Table 2-3, we can plot a family of curves for each company, as shown in Exhibits 2-1, 2-2, and 2-3. Using the calculations of Table 2-3, each exhibit's horizontal axis is the stock

Table 2-2. Relative volatility for stocks with listed options

Relative volatility range—%	Number of stocks
60 or less	14
65 — 75	39
80 — 90	77
95 — 105	90
110 — 120	59
125 — 135	38
140 — 150	33
155 — 165	9
170 or more	7
Total stocks	366

Note: Standard & Poor's 500 Stock Index relative volatility = 40
Source: *Value Line Options,* November 26, 1984.
Average stock = 100.

price divided by the option's exercise price; its vertical axis is the call price divided by the exercise price. Normalizing the data in this manner allows us to present all the available options on a single set of graphs. Thus, under- or overpriced calls can be quickly spotted by comparing their market prices with the normal curves.

Note that normal option premiums are extremely low for high-yielding Commonwealth Edison (about 5 percent for a six-month at-the-money call) and very high for volatile Datapoint (about 18 percent for six months). These wide variations are to be expected, given the differences in the stocks' yield and price volatility. However, one stock is not necessarily a better writing candidate than the others, even though I expect most writers would be enticed by the higher potential returns offered by Datapoint, the riskiest of the three examples.

RISK-REWARD ANALYSIS

Exhibits 2-4, 2-5, and 2-6 present risk-reward calculations and profit profiles for six-month covered-writing positions in the three selected companies.

Let's first look at the Boeing Company, Exhibit 2-4. Boeing common stock, having a 100 relative volatility and yielding 2.6 percent, is representative of an average stock available for covered writing. Trading at $55, at-the-money call

Table 2-3. Normal premiums for selected call options, November 1984

	Expiration month	Exercise price	Est. normal price	S/E	C/E
BOEING	Feb	60	1.71	.915	.028
		55	3.61	.998	.066
stock = $54.875		50	6.65	1.098	.133
yield = 2.6%		45	10.64	1.219	.236
RV = 100					
	May	60	3.02	.915	.050
		55	5.08	.998	.092
		50	7.97	1.098	.159
		45	11.63	1.219	.258
	Aug	60	3.95	.915	.066
		55	6.07	.998	.110
		50	8.91	1.098	.178
COMMONWEALTH EDISON	Feb	30	.17	.917	.006
		25	2.62	1.100	.105
		20	7.50	1.375	.375
stock = $27.50					
yield = 10.9%	May	30	.39	.917	.013
RV = 60		25	2.81	1.100	.112
		20	7.50	1.375	.375
	Aug	30	.58	.917	.019
		25	2.95	1.100	.118
DATAPOINT	Feb	20	.32	.719	.016
		15	1.56	.958	.104
stock = $14.375		10	4.90	1.438	.490
yield = nil					
RV = 160	May	20	.77	.719	.038
		15	2.29	.958	.153
		10	5.47	1.438	.547
	Aug	20	1.13	.719	.056
		15	2.79	.958	.186
		10	5.91	1.438	.591

Source: *Value Line Options,* November 26, 1984.

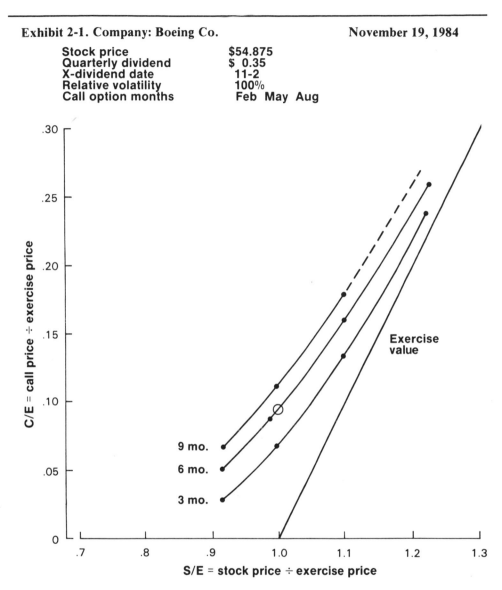

Exhibit 2-1. Company: Boeing Co. November 19, 1984

Stock price	**$54.875**
Quarterly dividend	**$ 0.35**
X-dividend date	**11-2**
Relative volatility	**100%**
Call option months	**Feb May Aug**

Y-axis: C/E = call price ÷ exercise price

X-axis: S/E = stock price ÷ exercise price

Exercise value

9 mo.
6 mo.
3 mo.

options are priced at $5, a 9.1 percent premium ($5 ÷ $55 = .091). Adding together the dividends ($70), the interest earned on the received option premium ($25), and the $500 option premium, we find that the covered-writing position offers a 10.8 percent ($595 ÷ $5,500 = .108) total precommission return for six months, if the stock ends up at $55 or higher. On the downside, the position

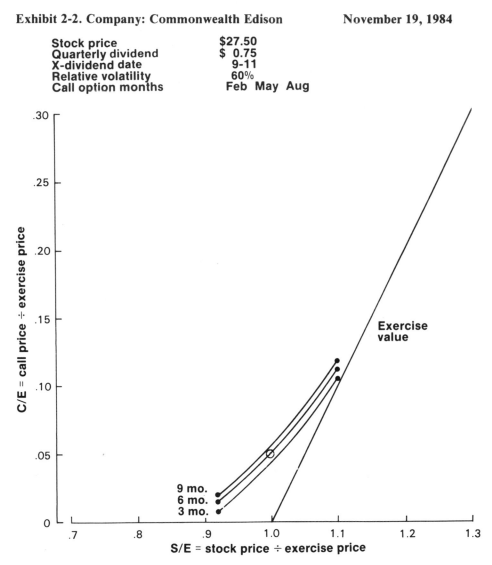

Exhibit 2-2. Company: Commonwealth Edison   November 19, 1984

Stock price	$27.50
Quarterly dividend	$ 0.75
X-dividend date	9-11
Relative volatility	60%
Call option months	Feb May Aug

would experience losses at future stock prices below its $49 break-even point. These risk-reward relationships are similar to the basic option example of Strategy 3, Chapter 1.

Covered-option writing can obviously reduce the risk of common stock ownership, but by what amount? Turning again to *Value Line Options*, we note that their estimated relative volatility for the covered writing position is only 50, or half the risk of the common stock. Therefore, a diversified portfolio

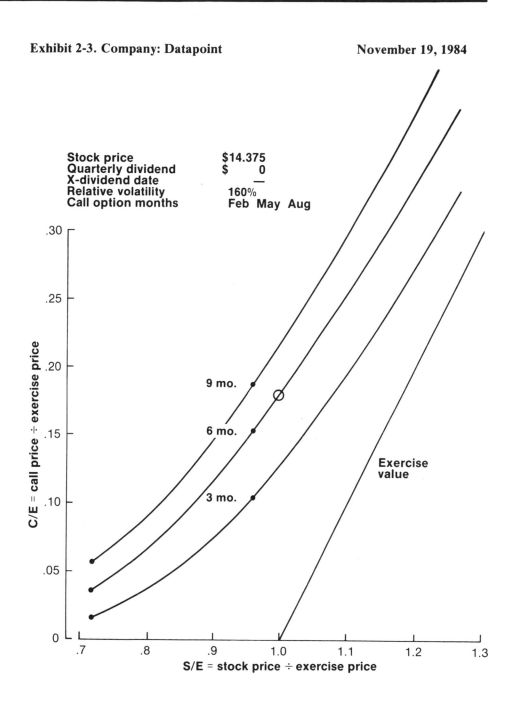

Exhibit 2-3. Company: Datapoint November 19, 1984

Stock price $14.375
Quarterly dividend $ 0
X-dividend date —
Relative volatility 160%
Call option months Feb May Aug

of covered-writing positions on average stocks like Boeing can be expected to provide long-term returns similar to a balanced portfolio of stocks and money market instruments. The profit profiles of Exhibits 2-4, 2-5, and 2-6 include this 50/50 stock/cash combination for comparison. As shown by the Boeing profit profile in Exhibit 2-4, the covered-writing-position is superior over a $46 to $64 future-stock-price range, but underperforms the stock/cash combination at greater up- or down-price movements. Covered writers who desire more risk reduction would use in-the-money and/or the nine-month August calls. Those who seek higher returns, at a correspondingly higher risk level, would use out-of-the-money and/or the shorter-term February calls.

Turn next to the Commonwealth Edison covered-writing position of Exhibit 2-5. With the stock at $27.50, there are no at-the-money calls available. The six-month choices are: an in-the-money $25 call trading at $2.75, and an out-of-the-money $30 call at $.375. I chose the $30 call for my example because in-the-money calls on high-yielding stocks are often exercised prematurely, just before an ex-dividend date. Thus, the seller of a Commonwealth Edison May 25 call could easily lose the stock's next $.75 quarterly dividend via assignment, and also incur roundtrip commission expenses for reinvesting the proceeds.

Although some option writers believe that any premium received when selling out-of-the-money calls on high-yielding stocks is "found money," I strongly disagree. Even though it is not volatile, Commonwealth Edison stock could, under certain market conditions, rise to well above the $30 exercise price over the next six months—it advanced over 30 percent, from $21.50 to $28.875, during 1984. Why give up this potential appreciation for the miniscule ⅜ call option premium?

The Datapoint example of Exhibit 2-6 is representative of covered-writing positions on highly speculative stocks. Trading at $14.50, Datapoint had declined from its all-time high of $67.50 in 1981 down to $10.875 in 1982, then rebounded to $30 in 1983, before dropping back to the $15 area in November 1984. Its relative volatility rating is very high, 160, but the sale of the slightly out-of-the-money $15 call option cuts the RV down to 80 for the covered-writing position, less than that of the average common stock.

THE COVERED-WRITING STRATEGIES LINE

As illustrated by the examples, selling call options against common stocks reduces the risk of stock ownership. An at-the-money call, for instance, cuts

Exhibit 2-4. Selling covered calls on Boeing Co.

	Prices at Expiration			
Stock	$ 30	$ 40	$ 55	$ 90
Call	0	0	0	35
Profit or (loss) on stock	(2500)	(1500)	0	3500
Profit or (loss) on call	500	500	500	(3000)
T-bill interest on $500	25	25	25	25
Dividends received	70	70	70	70
Total profit or (loss)	(1905)	(905)	595	595
Return on investment (ROI)	−34.6%	−16.5%	+10.8%	+10.8%

Stock = $55
Six-month, $55 call = 5.00 ($500)

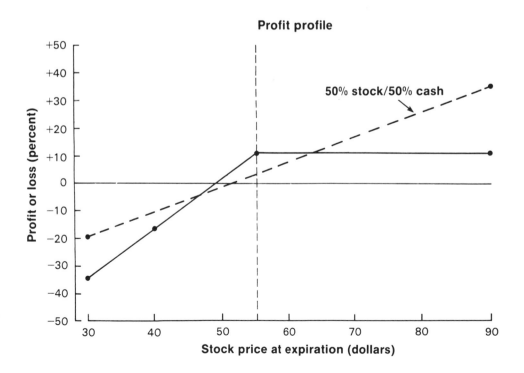

Profit profile

Exhibit 2-5. Selling covered calls on Commonwealth Edison

		Prices at Expiration			
		$ 20	$ 25	$ 30	$ 35
	Stock	$ 20	$ 25	$ 30	$ 35
	Call	0	0	0	5
Profit or (loss) on stock		(750)	(250)	250	750
Profit or (loss) on call		38	38	38	(462)
T-bill interest on $38		2	2	2	2
Dividends received		150	150	150	150
Total profit or (loss)		(560)	(60)	440	440
Return on investment (ROI)		−20.4%	− 2.2%	+16.0%	+16.0%

Stock = $27.50
Six-month, $30 call = .375 ($38)

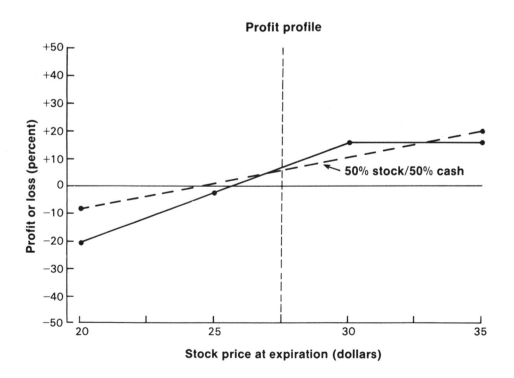

Profit profile

50% stock/50% cash

Profit or loss (percent)

Stock price at expiration (dollars)

Exhibit 2-6. Selling covered calls on Datapoint

		Prices at Expiration			
Stock		$ 5	$ 10	$ 15	$ 30
Call		0	0	0	15
Profit or (loss) on stock		(950)	(450)	50	1550
Profit or (loss) on call		225	225	225	(1275)
T-bill interest on $225		11	11	11	11
Dividends received		0	0	0	0
Total profit or (loss)		(714)	(214)	286	286
Return on investment (ROI)		−49.2%	−14.8%	+19.7%	+19.7%

Stock = $14.50
Six-month, $15 call = 2.25 ($225)

Profit profile

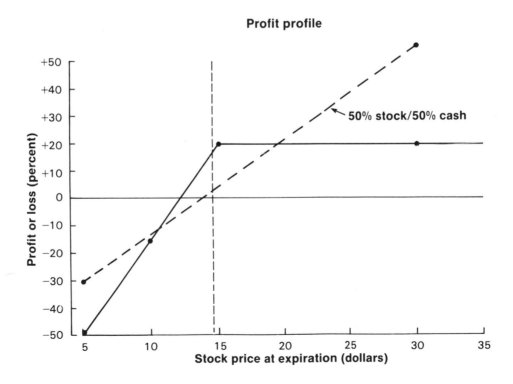

the risk roughly in half. Risk can be reduced even further by writing in-the-money calls. These risk-reward relationships are indicated by the covered-writing strategies line of Exhibit 2-7, a variation of the capital market line previously shown in the Introduction. The lower end of the line is risk-free money market instruments whereas the upper area is common stock. Covered-writing strategies fall between these extremes, illustrating how various option-selling strategies can alter the risk-reward characteristics of one's portfolio.

While on the subject of risk reduction, I must emphasize the importance of portfolio diversification. The relative volatility of the stock market, as measured by Standard & Poor's 500 stock index, for instance, is only about 40, a number far less than that of individual common stocks. It's even less than most individual covered-writing positions. Therefore, when true risk reduction is the objective, any covered-writing program should be based on a properly diversified portfolio of underlying common stocks.

The covered-writing strategies line of Exhibit 2-7 is based on normal option premiums and excludes brokerage commissions. Unless overpriced options are sold, commission expenses will reduce the strategy's profit potential with the net result of below-the-line performance. Since the same risk reduction can be achieved by simply combining commission-free money market instruments with one's stock portfolio, it makes little or no sense to sell normally priced calls. As you will soon see, professionally managed option-writing portfolios, whose huge sizes prevent them from taking advantage of small pockets of pricing inefficiencies, have achieved subpar performance.

PORTFOLIO MANAGEMENT

I recall a lengthy article about a retired investor whose major assets were in a covered-writing program that he personally managed. This investor maintained meticulous records, including daily charts for each security position. The article said he was pleased to supplement his corporate pension with the "premium income" earned through the sale of calls. The article was obviously intended to support the merits of covered writing; however, at the end, it casually mentioned that the investor admitted he could have achieved better results if he had not sold options. This retiree simply enjoyed spending several hours daily working on his portfolio; he voluntarily sacrificed performance for something to do with his time.

Successful investing is not a game; it's a serious business conducted in the world's most competitive arena—the U.S. securities markets. As an option

Exhibit 2-7. The covered-writing strategies line for common stocks having average risk

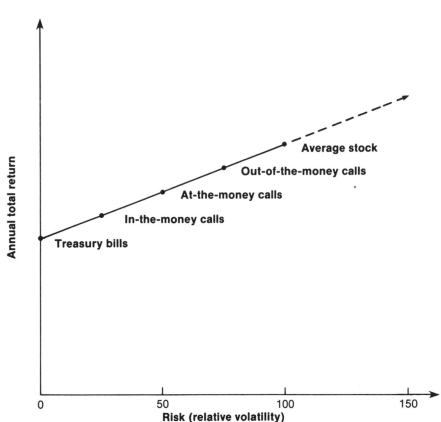

writer, you must match your wits with highly skilled professionals who are able to access data and other resources far beyond your reach. The only way to hold your own is to take advantage of market inefficiencies that are too small to attract the professionals' attention. The alternative is to hire skilled professionals to do the job for you; their management fees will usually be less than the higher commissions you will likely spend trying to compete with them on their home turf.

For those of you who wish to manage your own option writing portfolios, here are guidelines that should help you achieve better performance.

• Diversify your portfolio by owning at least twenty stocks, each in a different industry.

- Buy stocks you are willing to hold for the long term. In other words, do not buy a stock simply because it has an attractive option available at the moment; there will probably be times when you will choose to hold the stock unhedged.
- Own at least 200 shares of each stock. Commission expenses are exorbitant when trading single options.
- Sell calls that are overpriced. This generally means avoiding heavily traded options on popular stocks; institutional selling pressure will usually depress their premiums to levels of undervaluation.
- Minimize portfolio-turnover expenses by selling the longest-term calls, and plan to hold them until expiration—most stockbrokers urge sale of the shortest-term calls.
- Use carefully placed limit orders—*never* buy or sell at the market. Be prepared to change your limit price quickly, if the stock starts to move, or give this responsibility to your stockbroker.
- Do not let your calls be assigned against you. Although that particular transaction would be profitable, the extra commissions, due to both selling your stock and replacing it, will cancel out any profits you might earn over the long run. This advice may seem obvious, but it is surprising how many investors plan to let their stock be called away whenever an option ends up in-the-money. This is great for stockbrokers but hazardous to your wealth.
- Place option premiums received in money market instruments as a reserve for the later repurchase of those calls that end up in-the-money. Whether or not this reserve grows over time will let you know if your option-writing strategy is producing the extra returns you anticipated.
- Use margin only if you can employ it effectively for after-tax performance, and if you can also assume the extra risk.
- Manage your portfolio for long-term capital gains if your account is not exempt from income taxes. This is probably the most important reason for handling your own portfolio. Professionally managed option-writing programs will probably give you better pre-tax performance; however, since they are usually unconcerned with tax consequences, most of these programs' profits will be short-term.
- Recognize that buying back a losing in-the-money call produces a short-term capital loss which will offset short-term gains from other calls which expire without worth. This tactic will provide savings in both taxes and commissions as compared to letting your stock be called away.
- Review your performance periodically against appropriate market indexes like the S&P 500 combined with money market instruments—if you are not

beating the market averages you have no business being in an option-writing program. When calculating performance, make sure you include unrealized gains and losses so that you arrive at a true net-worth figure. I have seen instances where covered writers would go on for a year or more without taking any losses; they would let their profitable stocks be called away and hold their losers. Some covered writers actually experienced declining net worth in their account at the same time they believed they were earning extra income and were paying taxes on their illusory profits.

DOES COVERED WRITING REALLY WORK?

Any successful investment strategy must be based on sound financial principles. It is also helpful if the experience of professionals who employ the proposed strategy is attainable, verifiable, and currently meaningful. Historical performance data for strategies out of the market's mainstream, however, are usually not available to most investors. The data that is made available is often done so for sales purposes only, and can be deceptive.

When listed call options first began trading in 1973, it was obvious to knowledgeable investors that premiums were excessive. Covered-call writing offered high risk-adjusted returns but, lacking the track records of others, most investors were reluctant to venture into the strategy. As successful performance was demonstrated during the ensuing years, however, more and more "smart money" moved into covered writing. The additional selling pressure naturally depressed the premium levels.

Undaunted by the low option premiums prevailing at the time (1977), several mutual funds were marketed, based on the successful experience of others during the early years of abnormally high premiums. A review of their performance follows.

HISTORICAL PERFORMANCE DATA FOR COVERED CALL WRITING

Selling covered call options does reduce stock-ownership risk by the premiums received. Can the strategy, however, produce higher returns at less risk, as proponents continually claim? Stated another way, does covered call writing produce risk-adjusted rates of return *above* the covered-writing strategies line of Exhibit 2-7, after the deduction of management fees, administrative expenses, and trading costs? Let's turn to the professional option writers' public track records for the answer.

One no-load and five full-load option-writing mutual funds were introduced to the investment public in 1977, each with the promising term "income" in its name. All six funds talked of high returns at below-average risk. Returns of 12 to 15 percent were commonly promised at a time when long-term stock market returns were about 9 percent and money market funds were yielding 6 percent. Some overzealous sales representatives even touted returns of 15 to 20 percent—or higher. One fund—Federated Option Income Fund—dropped out four years later. The remaining five have flourished, growing from about $300 million in 1977 to $2.5 billion in total assets at the end of 1984.

In my book *Advanced Investment Strategies* (Dow Jones-Irwin, 1978), I ventured a contrary opinion on how the funds would perform: "I believe these funds will achieve only their 12- to 15-percent objective during the bull phase of a market cycle, and then only if they don't trade their positions too frequently. They will do worse in a sideways market, and they will be losers in bear markets. Over a market cycle, I doubt that they will even match the average return from risk-free money market instruments." Let's evaluate these funds' performance (and my prediction).

Portfolio reviews over the years showed that the funds' risk-levels were somewhat higher than the center of the covered-writing strategies line: most of their common stock holdings had above-average volatility, options sold were usually at- or out-of-the-money, and, at times, stocks were held with no calls written against them. For comparison with market indexes, and to give them the benefit of any doubt (since I am obviously biased against them), I will assume their risk-reward postures were the same as a lower-risk balanced portfolio containing 50 percent S&P type common stocks and 50 percent Treasury bills—the middle of the covered-writing strategies line.

As shown by the analysis of Table 2-4, all five funds underperformed the S&P 500/T-bill performance-evaluation standard—their 7.5-year total returns ranged from 87 percent to 108 percent compared to 124 percent for the average of the two market indexes (143 percent for the S&P 500 and 105 percent for Treasury bills). The 102 percent average for the five, less than risk-free money market returns, was even lower than I expected, given the favorable market environment for writing calls during that time period. The past 7.5 years, involving a steadily rising stock market, was an ideal period for covered call writing; the funds have yet to experience a bear market.

Be aware that a 102 percent total return over 7.5 years is only a 9.8 percent *compounded annual rate of return,* the proper method for reporting results for any investment strategy; some might claim 13.6 percent, incorrectly obtained by dividing 102 percent by 7.5.

Note from Table 2-4 that, contrary to popular belief, covered writing does not produce high returns in sideways stock markets—the funds underperformed Treasury bills in each of the static years. *Covered writing is a bull market strategy!*

In my opinion, the funds should have at least matched the 124 percent return earned by the lower-risk S&P 500/T-bill combination. While I expected them to underperform risk-free Treasury bills over a market cycle, they should have done much better in a rising stock market. Perhaps these funds are so large that they are forced to accept underpriced calls; or perhaps, in addition to their administrative expenses and management fees, they incurred excessive trading costs by turning their portfolios over too frequently. They certainly have not lived up to expectations, yet they continue to attract new investors lured both by sales reps pitching high "current income" and by uninformed financial writers applauding the funds' merits.

Here are other factors that should be recognized by anyone considering an option income fund purchase. Although the sales inducement of an option income fund is high current income, its definition of "income" includes short-term capital gains from option trades, an income source dependent on favorable market conditions. Its *real* income (investment income) from dividends received, minus operating expenses, is only about 3 percent. In addition, in an apparent effort to sustain the high-income illusion during poor market years, some of these option income funds have been realizing short-term capital gains, while retaining long-term loss positions. Consequently, net asset values per share at the end of 1984 were as much as 30 percent below what they started at in 1977. Not only are fund buyers not truly earning the high "income" received, *they are also paying taxes at ordinary income rates on the return of their own capital.*

Writing calls against common stocks cannot be expected to enhance investment performance over the long run. Even when overpriced calls can be found, trading expenses are likely to eradicate any advantage gained. However, winning option strategies are available to astute, noninstitutional-sized investors. They include puts and calls in combination with undervalued convertible securities. I will present these advanced investment strategies in this book.

Table 2-4. Mutual funds specializing in covered call option writing

	6 mo.	Annual returns—percent							7.5 year total return
	1977	1978	1979	1980	1981	1982	1983	1984	
Colonial	+ 1.0	+ 6.5	+16.9	+17.8	+ 0.8	+11.3	+17.9	+ 3.7	103%
Gateway	----	+ 5.9	+14.6	+15.1	+ 4.2	+ 8.5	+14.2	+ 3.6	87
Kemper	+ 0.2	+ 1.8	+16.5	+23.5	+ 2.6	+13.5	+15.6	+ 5.2	108
Oppenheimer	+ 0.9	+ 6.5	+10.6	+13.3	+13.2	+14.5	+15.5	+ 2.1	106
Putnam	+ 1.1	+ 5.9	+14.2	+17.8	+ 3.1	+16.1	+13.5	+ 4.9	105
Average	+ 0.8	+ 5.3	+14.6	+17.5	+ 4.8	+12.8	+15.3	+ 3.9	102
S&P 500	– 3.1	+ 6.5	+18.4	+32.5	– 5.0	+21.6	+22.5	+ 6.2	143
T-bills	+ 2.8	+ 7.1	+10.0	+11.4	+14.2	+10.9	+ 8.9	+9.9	105
50% S&P/ 50% T-bills	– 0.1	+ 6.8	+14.2	+22.0	+ 4.6	+16.2	+15.7	+ 8.0	124

Source: Standard & Poor's
Notes: 1. Gateway Option Income Fund is no-load; the other four are full-load.
             2. Performance results do not include sales commissions of up to 9.3 percent on the funds invested.

CHAPTER 3

Basic Index-Option Strategies

Broad-based index options have become the most popular securities introduced by the financial community in recent years. These unique instruments, available on a number of different stock-market averages, have made it possible for speculators and hedgers alike to take put- and call-option positions directly on the market. This advantage eliminates both time delays inherent in analyzing and monitoring strategies on individual stocks, and high commission costs when executing a large number of small stock option orders.

Broad-based index options recently available:

American Stock Exchange

- Amex Major Market Index (XMI)
- Amex Market Value Index (XAM)

Chicago Board Options Exchange

- Standard & Poor's 100 Index (OEX)
- Standard & Poor's 500 Index (SPX)

New York Stock Exchange

- NYSE Composite Index (NYA)
- NYSE Double Index (NDX)

Pacific Stock Exchange

- Pacific Stock Exchange Technology Index (PSE)

Philadelphia Stock Exchange

- Value Line Composite Index (XVL)
- National Over-the-Counter Index (XOC)

Of the nine broad-based indexes: the movements of five will reflect those of large capitalization companies (XMI, OEX, SPX, NYA, and NDX); three are closely related to the price movements of secondary (small-capitalization) companies (XAM, PSE and XOC); and the unweighted Value Line Index, based on 1,700 issues, cuts across both categories. The proper option choice for those using index puts and calls will depend on their market forecasts if they are speculating, the type of stocks held in their portfolios if they are hedging, and available premiums in either scenario.

INDEX-OPTION PREMIUMS AND PRICE CURVES

Premiums on index options are influenced by the same variables affecting premiums on stock options. However, the underlying security's price volatility is a major difference between the two option families, one that those experienced with stock options may have difficulty with at first. By definition, the average stock has a relative volatility (RV) of 100. Three- and six-month calls on average-risk stocks, such as the Boeing example in Chapter 2, will typically trade at premiums of about 6–7 percent and 9–10 percent, respectively. Market indexes exhibit much lower price volatility than individual stocks; their RVs are usually below 50. Thus, index-option premiums can be expected to be far lower than those of stock options.

Tables 3-1 and 3-2 present *Value Line's* February 1985 estimates of normal premiums for the Chicago Board Option Exchange's exceptionally popular OEX puts and calls. Named Standard & Poor's 100 Stock Index, this market indicator was designed to closely track the traditional S&P 500, generally

Table 3-1. Estimated normal premiums for S&P 100 index call options

	Expiration month	Exercise price	Estimated normal price	I/E*	C/E†
	Mar	195	.10	.913	.0005
		190	.30	.937	.0016
Index = 177.97		185	.85	.962	.0046
Yield = 4.3%		180	2.15	.989	.0119
RV = 45		175	4.84	1.017	.0277
T-bills = 8.25%		170	8.64	1.047	.0508
		165	13.19	1.079	.0799
		160	18.04	1.112	.1128
		155	22.99	1.148	.1483
	Apr	195	.86	.913	.0044
		190	1.54	.937	.0081
		185	2.68	.962	.0145
		180	4.47	.989	.0248
		175	7.03	1.017	.0402
		170	10.36	1.047	.0609
		165	14.31	1.079	.0867
		160	18.70	1.112	.1169
		155	23.36	1.148	.1507
	May	195	1.44	.913	.0074
		190	2.31	.937	.0122
		185	3.63	.962	.0196
		180	5.51	.989	.0306
		175	8.05	1.017	.0460
		170	11.24	1.047	.0661
		165	15.00	1.079	.0909
		160	19.20	1.112	.1200
		155	23.69	1.148	.1528

*I/E = Index price ÷ Exercise price
†C/E = Call price ÷ Exercise price

Source: *Value Line Options,* February 25, 1985.

Table 3-2. Estimated normal premiums for S&P 100 index put options

	Expiration month	Exercise price	Estimated normal price	I/E*	P/E†
	Mar	195	17.05	.913	.0874
		190	12.13	.937	.0638
Index = 177.97		185	7.46	.962	.0403
Yield = 4.3%		180	3.56	.989	.0198
RV = 45		175	1.23	1.017	.0070
T-bills = 8.25%		170	.34	1.047	.0020
		165	.09	1.079	.0005
		160	.02	1.112	.0001
		155	.01	1.148	.0001
	Apr	195	17.41	.913	.0893
		190	12.85	.937	.0676
		185	8.75	.962	.0473
		180	5.40	.989	.0300
		175	3.00	1.017	.0171
		170	1.54	1.047	.0091
		165	.75	1.079	.0045
		160	.36	1.112	.0022
		155	.17	1.148	.0011
	May	195	17.85	.913	.0915
		190	13.52	.937	.0712
		185	9.67	.962	.0523
		180	6.48	.989	.0360
		175	4.07	1.017	.0233
		170	2.42	1.047	.0142
		165	1.38	1.079	.0084
		160	.77	1.112	.0048
		155	.43	1.148	.0028

*I/E = Index price ÷ Exercise price
†P/E = Put price ÷ Exercise price

Source: *Value Line Options,* February 25, 1985.

considered to be the best measurement of the high-quality sector of the stock market.

Exhibits 3-1 and 3-2 provide families of curves for S&P 100 index options having expirations ranging from one to three months (longer term options did not exist at the time). As provided by the calculations of Tables 3-1 and 3-2, each exhibit's horizontal axis is the index's price divided by the option's

Exhibit 3-1. Standard & Poor's 100 index call-option curves February 1985

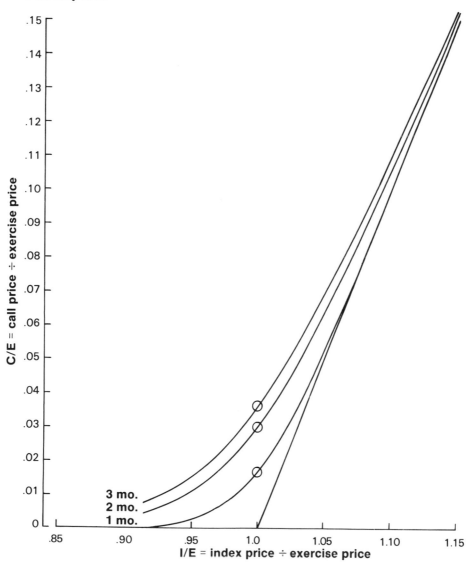

**Exhibit 3-2. Standard & Poor's 100 index put-option curves
February 1985**

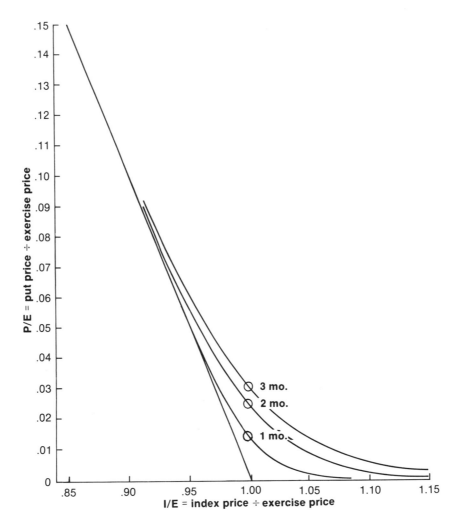

exercise price (I/E); its vertical axis is the option price divided by the exercise price (C/E for calls and P/E for puts). Thus the data, normalized as it was for individual stock options in Chapter 2, allows presentation of all available puts or calls on single sets of graphs.

As shown in Exhibit 3-1, S&P 100 index calls trading at-the-money (I/E = 1.0) and having three months life were expected to trade at a 3.7 percent premium (C/E = .037). At-the-money three-month index puts were expected to trade at a 3 percent premium (P/E = .030), as shown in Exhibit 3-2.

Actual prices at the time found the calls to be selling close to the estimates, but the puts were considerably lower. Since it is generally believed that call premiums are determined by supply and demand and that premiums for the less popular puts are kept in line through the conversion process, professionals apparently found it more difficult to execute index-option conversions than stock-option conversions. To take advantage of low-index put premiums, converters must buy puts, sell calls, and own the market, a strategy much more complex and capital-intensive than combining puts and calls with individual common stocks. This might indicate that pockets of pricing inefficiencies are more likely to be found with index options than with stock options.

BASIC INDEX-OPTION STRATEGIES

Chapter 1 presented seven basic strategies involving puts, calls, and common stocks. Each of those strategies can be duplicated with index options. In place of individual stocks, we can substitute a properly diversified stock portfolio or an index fund which owns all the stocks making up the index. The seven basic index-option strategies, using three-month index puts and calls, are presented in Exhibits 3-3 through 3-9; index put- and call-option straddles are presented in Exhibits 3-10 and 3-11.

Over the last five to ten years high-quality stock portfolios like the S&P 500 have yielded about 5 percent with money market instruments at about 10 percent. The risk-reward calculation tables are based on assumptions which reflect recent market years as follows:

- The index is at 200, a round number for ease of illustration and a price level comparable to most indexes as they were trading in 1985.

- Since a single option represents $20,000 worth of the index, a stock portfolio (or index fund) worth $20,000 is held long or sold short—the calculations assume that the portfolio's future price action will precisely match the index's.

- The stock portfolio pays dividends of $250 every three months (5 percent annual yield).

- A three-month call option, having a $200 exercise price, is trading at $7.50 ($750 for each at-the-money call on $20,000 worth of stock).

- A three-month put option, also having a $200 exercise price, is trading at $5 ($500 for each at-the-money put on $20,000 worth of stock).

- Unused funds, or premiums received from option sales, are placed in U.S. government Treasury bills (or a money market fund) yielding 10 percent (2.5 percent for three months).
- Each position is held until the options expire (three months).

Each strategy is evaluated by a risk-reward analysis for index prices of 180, 200, and 220 three months later when the options expire, a range that will encompass most three-month price movements for a low-volatility market average. Be alert to the fact, however, that even a high-quality index like the S&P 500 will occasionally experience price moves greater than 10 percent in three months. A profit profile follows each risk-reward calculation table, similar to the illustrations for stock options in Chapter 1.

Again, I excluded brokerage commissions and income tax consequences for ease of illustration; however, investors must always take these critical factors into consideration before selecting any investment strategy. Be aware that, under current tax law, index options are taxed differently than stock options. The gains and losses, both actually realized and deemed realized for tax purposes (by virtue of being marked to market at year end), are aggregated. The net gain or loss is then treated as 60 percent long-term capital gain or loss and 40 percent short-term capital gain or loss. Also, if the underlying stock portfolio is expected to "mimic" the market, as I assumed for the examples, the use of index options might terminate the stocks' holding periods depending on future IRS regulations. You should consult your tax advisor before employing any strategy involving index puts and calls.

Since the risk-reward characteristics are similar to the stock option strategies of Chapter 1, I will not discuss each of them individually. I do urge you, however, to study the examples carefully. It is my belief that index puts and calls are far more useful tools than individual stock options for both conservative investors hedging their stock portfolios and speculators betting on overall market movements. They provide: better liquidity (tighter bid-ask price spreads), lower brokerage commissions, underpriced and overpriced opportunities, and more predictable price action relative to overall market movements.

But be sure to recognize that, unless your stock portfolio can be expected to reflect the market, the purchase of a protective index put or the sale of an index call may not give you the results you are seeking—there will likely be divergences between the future price action of your stock portfolio and the market index. Divergence, of course, can work to your advantage, just as it may work against you. If you are a good stock picker, you will do better than the examples shown, since your stock selections will provide greater upside returns and/or less downside risk than the market. You will also do better than the examples if you purchase underpriced options and/or sell overpriced options.

As you will see in the final chapters on SuperHedging, index puts and calls can be valuable tools for protecting portfolios that are expected to outperform the overall markets. They are revolutionary financial instruments that can enhance risk-adjusted returns.

Exhibit 3-3. Basic index-option strategies 10 and 10a

	Price	*Prices at Expiration (3 months)*		
Index (stock)	$ 200.00	$ 180	$ 200	$ 220
Call	7.50	0	0	20
Put	5.00	20	0	0

Strategy 10: Buy stock

Profit or (loss) on stock	(2000)	0	2000
Dividends received	250	250	250
Total profit or (loss)	(1750)	250	2250

Strategy 10a: Buy one call and sell one put

Profit or (loss) on call	(750)	(750)	1250
Profit or (loss) on put	(1500)	500	500
T-bill interest on $19,750	495	495	495
Total profit or (loss)	(1755)	245	2245

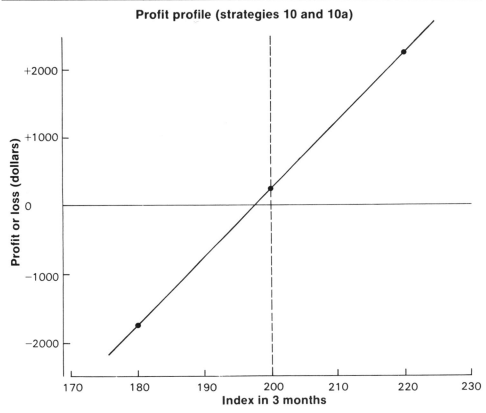

Profit profile (strategies 10 and 10a)

Exhibit 3-4. Basic index-option strategies 11 and 11a

	Price	Prices at Expiration (3 months)		
Index (stock)	$ 200.00	$ 180	$ 200	$ 220
Call	7.50	0	0	20
Put	5.00	20	0	0

Strategy 11: Buy stock and buy one put

Profit or (loss) on stock	(2000)	0	2000
Profit or (loss) on put	1500	(500)	(500)
Interest charge on $500	(15)	(15)	(15)
Dividends received	250	250	250
Total profit or (loss)	(265)	(265)	1735

Strategy 11a: Buy one call

Profit or (loss) on call	(750)	(750)	1250
T-bill interest on $19,250	480	480	480
Total profit or (loss)	(270)	(270)	1730

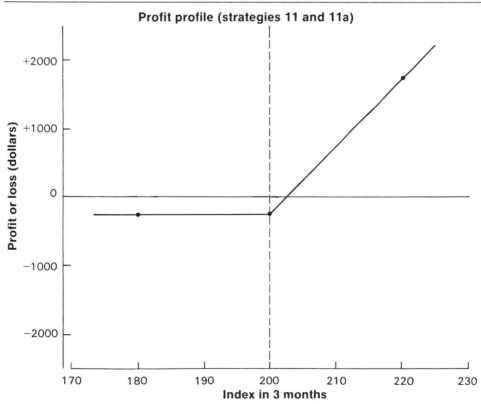

Profit profile (strategies 11 and 11a)

Exhibit 3-5. Basic index-option strategies 12 and 12a

	Price	*Prices at Expiration (3 months)*		
Index (stock)	$ 200.00	$ 180	$ 200	$ 220
Call	7.50	0	0	20
Put	5.00	20	0	0

Strategy 12: Buy stock and sell one call

Profit or (loss) on stock		(2000)	0	2000
Profit or (loss) on call		750	750	(1250)
T-bill interest on $750		20	20	20
Dividends received		250	250	250
Total profit or (loss)		(980)	1020	1020

Strategy 12a: Sell one put

Profit or (loss) on put		(1500)	500	500
T-bill interest on $20,500		515	515	515
Total profit or (loss)		(985)	1015	1015

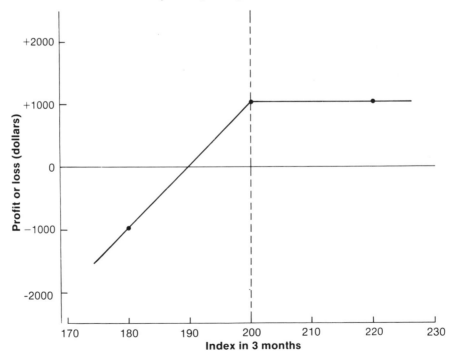

Profit profile (strategies 12 and 12a)

Exhibit 3-6. Basic index-option strategies 13 and 13a

	Price	*Prices at Expiration (3 months)*		
Index (stock)	$ 200.00	$ 180	$ 200	$ 220
Call	7.50	0	0	20
Put	5.00	20	0	0

Strategy 13: Buy stock, buy one put, and sell one call

Profit or (loss) on stock	(2000)	0	2000
Profit or (loss) on put	1500	(500)	(500)
Profit or (loss) on call	750	750	(1250)
T-bill interest on $250	5	5	5
Dividends received	250	250	250
Total profit or (loss)	505	505	505

Strategy 13a: Buy Treasury bills

T-bill interest on $20,000	500	500	500

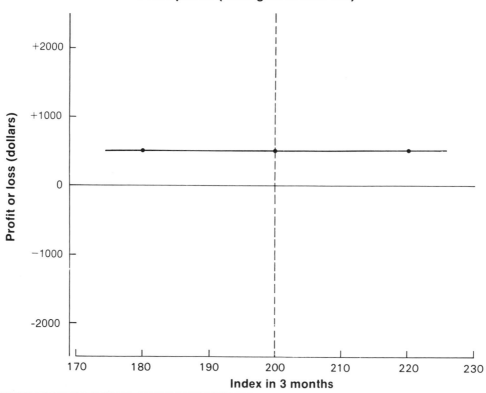

Profit profile (strategies 13 and 13a)

Exhibit 3-7. Basic index-option strategies 14 and 14a

	Price	Prices at Expiration (3 months)		
Index (stock)	$ 200.00	$ 180	$ 200	$ 220
Call	7.50	0	0	20
Put	5.00	20	0	0

Strategy 14: Short stock and sell one put

Profit or (loss) on stock	2000	0	(2000)
Profit or (loss) on put	(1500)	500	500
T-bill interest on $20,050	515	515	515
Dividends paid	(250)	(250)	(250)
Total profit or (loss)	765	765	(1235)

Strategy 14a: Sell one call

Profit or (loss) on call	750	750	(1250)
T-bill interest on $20,750	520	520	520
Total profit or (loss)	1270	1270	(730)

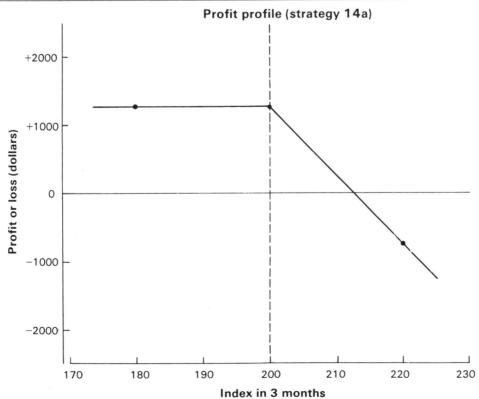

Profit profile (strategy 14a)

Exhibit 3-8. Basic index-option strategies 15 and 15a

	Price	*Prices at Expiration (3 months)*		
Index (stock)	$ 200.00	$ 180	$ 200	$ 220
Call	7.50	0	0	20
Put	5.00	20	0	0

Strategy 15: Short stock and buy one call

Profit or (loss) on stock	2000	0	(2000)
Profit or (loss) on call	(750)	(750)	1250
T-bill interest on $19,250	480	480	480
Dividends paid	(250)	(250)	(250)
Total profit or (loss)	1480	(520)	(520)

Strategy 15a: Buy one put

Profit or (loss) on put	1500	(500)	(500)
T-bill interest on $19,500	485	485	485
Total profit or (loss)	1985	(15)	(15)

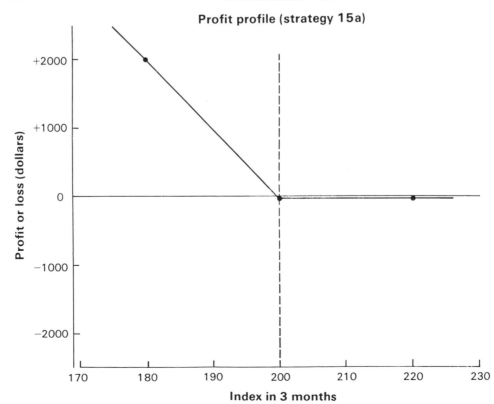

Profit profile (strategy 15a)

Exhibit 3-9. Basic index-option strategies 16 and 16a

	Price	*Prices at Expiration (3 months)*		
Index (stock)	$ 200.00	$ 180	$ 200	$ 220
Call	7.50	0	0	20
Put	5.00	20	0	0

Strategy 16: Short stock

Profit or (loss) on stock	2000	0	(2000)
T-bill interest on $20,000	500	500	500
Dividends paid	(250)	(250)	(250)
Total profit or (loss)	2250	250	(1750)

Strategy 16a: Buy one put and sell one call

Profit or (loss) on put	1500	(500)	(500)
Profit or (loss) on call	750	750	(1250)
T-bill interest on $20,250	505	505	505
Total profit or (loss)	2755	755	(1245)

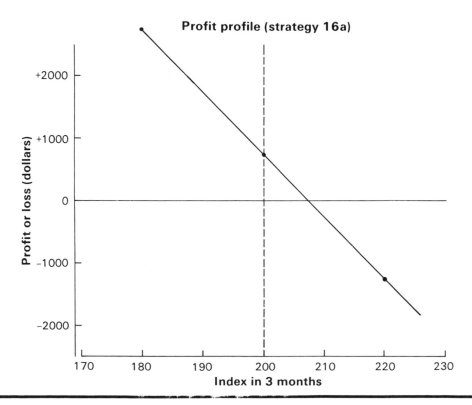

Profit profile (strategy 16a)

Exhibit 3-10. Index-option strategies 17 and 17a

	Price	Prices at Expiration (3 months)		
Index (stock)	$ 200.00	$ 180	$ 200	$ 220
Call	7.50	0	0	20
Put	5.00	20	0	0

Strategy 17: Buy stock and sell two calls

Profit or (loss) on stock	(2000)	0	2000
Profit or (loss) on calls	1500	1500	(2500)
T-bill interest on $1,500	35	35	35
Dividends paid	250	250	250
Total profit or (loss)	(215)	1785	(215)

Strategy 17a: Sell one put and sell one call

Profit or (loss) on put	(1500)	500	500
Profit or (loss) on call	750	750	(1250)
T-bill interest on $21,250	530	530	530
Total profit or (loss)	(220)	1780	(220)

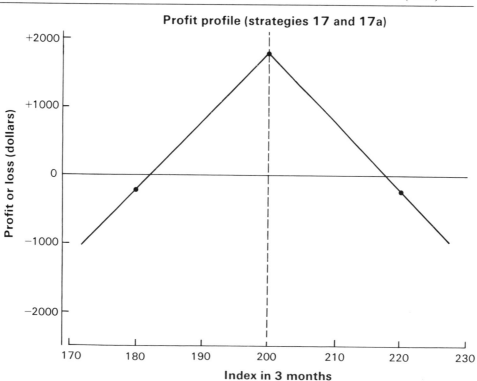

Profit profile (strategies 17 and 17a)

Exhibit 3-11. Index-option strategies 18 and 18a

	Price	Prices at Expiration (3 months)		
Index (stock)	$ 200.00	$ 180	$ 200	$ 220
Call	7.50	0	0	20
Put	5.00	20	0	0

Strategy 18: Buy stock and buy two puts

Profit or (loss) on stock		(2000)	0	2000
Profit or (loss) on puts		3000	(1000)	(1000)
Interest charge on $1,000		(25)	(25)	(25)
Dividends received		250	250	250
Total profit or (loss)		1225	(775)	1225

Strategy 18a: Buy one put and buy one call

Profit or (loss) on put		1500	(500)	(500)
Profit or (loss) on call		(750)	(750)	1250
T-bill interest on $18,750		470	470	470
Total profit or (loss)		1220	(780)	1220

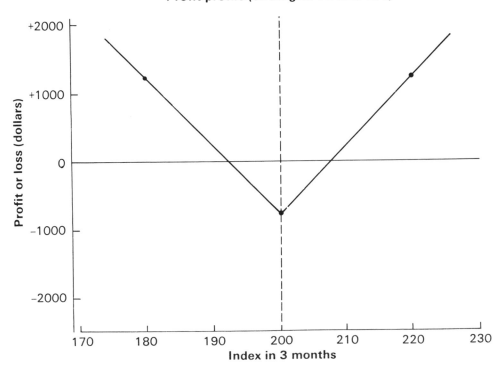

Profit profile (strategies 18 and 18a)

Profit or loss (dollars)

Index in 3 months

TRADITIONAL CONVERTIBLE BOND HEDGING STRATEGIES

CHAPTER 4

Identifying Undervalued Convertibles

In the introductory chapter, I stressed that successful hedging must involve either undervalued or overpriced stock-related securities. Examples included overpriced call options sold against common stock and normally valued calls sold against undervalued convertible bonds. Common stocks are always assumed to be fairly priced when analyzed as part of any hedging strategy. If this assumption is correct, fairly valued puts and calls in combination with common stocks can produce only subpar results after deducting trading expenses. It is mathematically improbable to achieve above-average returns when combining normally valued securities. This may be hard for option strategists to accept, but the laws of probability cannot be dismissed. If you have any doubt, review the poor results achieved by professional money managers writing covered calls against common stock holdings (Chapter 2).

Many investors, or their stockbrokers, believe their ability to pick undervalued common stocks allows them to earn excess returns through the sale of normally priced calls. Although that may be possible, it's a feat that has not been accomplished by professional option writers. If the pros can't do it, what chance does the nonprofessional investor have? I am not an adamant believer in efficient markets. I suspect, however, that, given the time and attention paid to them, if any market sector is efficiently priced, it is stocks having listed options. Investors with the ability to locate undervalued stocks are scouting areas other than those followed closely by Wall Street analysts. I'm sure that those who can find undervalued stocks are not inclined to limit their profits by selling covered calls.

There is a way, however, to locate undervalued securities right in the heart of Wall Street: the convertible securities market, a niche largely avoided by the money management fraternity because it lacks the liquidity needed for investing huge pools of capital. This chapter introduces carefully-selected convertible bonds as the primary instrument upon which a successful hedging program can be founded.

THE CONVERTIBLE ALTERNATIVE

Convertible bonds and convertible preferred stocks are hybrid securities. Like a straight (nonconvertible) bond, a convertible bond provides guaranteed interest (its coupon) and a maturity date when the issuing company must redeem it at par value (usually $1,000). In addition, the issuing company makes a third promise: at the bondholder's option, the company will exchange (convert) it for a stated number of common stock shares. Hence, a convertible bond will participate in future price advances by its underlying common stock while simultaneously providing the benefits of fixed income and safety. Convertible preferreds have similar characteristics, except they do not usually have redemption dates.

Viewed as alternative investments to their underlying stocks, most convertibles provide more income and less risk. The trade-off for safety and higher yield is usually less capital appreciation than their stocks upon a price advance. These risk-reward characteristics may be evaluated to determine whether a convertible is fairly priced, underpriced, or overpriced.

THE NEW-ISSUE CONVERTIBLE BOND MARKET

Convertible bonds and convertible preferreds are used by many companies to raise working capital or finance the acquisition of other companies. International

Business Machines (IBM), for example, acquired Rolm Corporation in 1984 via a AAA-rated, $1.3 billion convertible bond issue, the largest to date.

For analytic purposes, I have divided the convertible bond market into two categories: low-risk and aggressive. By my definition, *low-risk* convertibles are those issued by average- and above-average-quality companies; they must have underlying stocks rated B+ or higher by Standard & Poor's and New York Stock Exchange listing. Other convertibles, mostly issued by secondary companies, are placed in the *aggressive* category. Table 4-1 presents data showing representative convertible bonds of both types brought to the market in recent years.

Note the difference in issue size, $100 million versus $20 million. Low-risk convertibles typically have better market liquidity and are usually New York Stock Exchange listed, as are their underlying stocks. Aggressive convertibles may also trade on the New York Exchange but are frequently found on the American Stock Exchange or the over-the-counter market.

Notice also the difference in yield advantage (4 percent versus 10 percent) and conversion premium (15 percent versus 25 percent). Most new issues have a mixture of these characteristics and, once trading commences, the relationships will change as prices rise or fall in the trading aftermarkets. Convertibles cover the entire market spectrum, thereby allowing investors with different risk tolerances to construct portfolios that meet their specific investment objectives.

Hedging strategies may use either low-risk or aggressive convertibles, as I will show later. However, since the best opportunities are usually found in the lower-quality issues, I chose a convertible bond having the aggressive characteristics of Table 4-1 for the illustrations to follow. Let me emphasize that, when dealing with low-quality companies, convertible bonds should be favored

Table 4-1. Typical new convertible bond issues

	Low-risk	*Aggressive*
Price	$1,000	$1,000
Issue size, $ million	100	20
Interest rate (coupon)	8%	10%
Underlying common stock yield	4%	0%
Yield advantage	4%	10%
S&P investment grade	A	B
Straight bond equivalent yield	12%	16%
Investment value	$700	$650
Investment value premium	43%	54%
Conversion premium	15%	25%

over convertible preferreds. A company can skip a preferred dividend, but missing a bond interest payment is a far more serious matter that will be avoided if at all possible.

Let's now review the major factors that determine the market price for a hypothetical XYZ Corporation convertible bond: investment value and conversion value.

THE ANATOMY OF A CONVERTIBLE BOND

Investment value, shown as the horizontal line of Exhibit 4-1, is the price at which the bond would be expected to trade if it did not provide the conversion privilege. Bond-rating services estimate convertibles' investment values the same way they evaluate straight bonds: They consider inherent quality and prevailing interest rates for similar securities. Standard & Poor's, for example, assigns a AAA rating to the highest-quality bonds, like IBM's, and a D rating to those in default. Considering a Standard & Poor's investment grade of B for our example, and a 16 percent interest rate environment for similar, low-quality, twenty-year bonds (the straight bond equivalent yield of Table 4-1), an investment value of 65 ($650) would be computed. Thus, 65 becomes a "floor" that should support the convertible in the event of a price decline by its common stock. This "floor," however, is not fixed. It will drop if interest rates rise or the company's fundamentals deteriorate. It will rise if interest rates fall, if the fundamentals improve, and (since it must reach 100 on the maturity date) with the passage of time. Priced at 100, the convertible bond is trading at a 54 percent premium above its investment value ($100 \div 65 = 1.54$).

Conversion value, shown as the sloping straight line of Exhibit 4-1, is the bond's worth if it were exchanged for common stock and the shares were immediately sold. The straight line graph is determined by multiplying the conversion ratio (40 shares) by the common stock's price. At a current stock price of $20, for instance, the conversion value is 80 (40 shares × $20 per share = $800). Priced at 100, the convertible bond is trading at a 25 percent premium above its conversion value ($100 \div 80 = 1.25$).

The convertible bond's price of 100, representing a 54 percent investment value premium and a 25 percent conversion value premium, is the market's current appraisal of the bond's worth. The convertible price curve of Exhibit 4-1 is a prediction of future bond prices at any future stock price over the near term. The forecast is necessarily limited to the near term because the investment

Exhibit 4-1. The convertible price curve
XYZ Corp. 10 percent, 20-year bond trading at 100
* conversion ratio = 40 shares
* straight bond equivalent yield = 16 percent

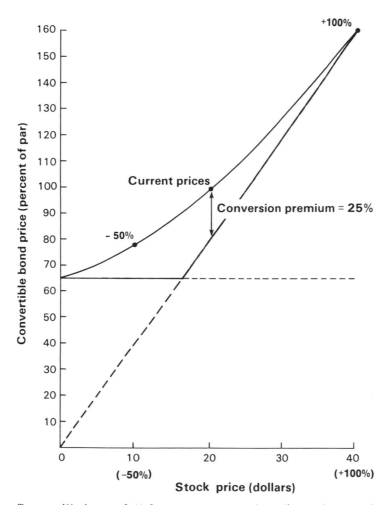

floor will rise or fall for reasons stated earlier, whereas the convertible price curve assumes a constant floor.

As shown by the bond's estimated price curve, if the common stock were to double from $20 to $40 the bond will advance 60 percent from 100 to 160, at which point we would expect it to be trading on its conversion value line. If the stock were to drop in half to $10, we would estimate a 22 percent bond decline to 78. Having these price projections, we can now proceed to a risk-reward analysis that evaluates the convertible bond as an alternative to its underlying common stock.

NEW-ISSUE RISK-REWARD ANALYSIS

The XYZ Corporation 10-percent convertible bond was representative of new issues offered by secondary companies in recent years of high interest rates. How did the convertible compare with the purchase of the nondividend-paying XYZ common stock? Assuming a one-year holding period, and adding the bond's 10 percent yield to expected capital gains or losses, a risk-reward comparison is shown by Table 4-2.

The convertible bond offered nearly three-fourths the upside potential of its common at only one-fourth the downside risk, while returning 10 percent more in a static market. As attractive as these numbers appear, they are, in fact, representative of most newly-issued convertibles.

New-issue convertibles, both low-risk and aggressive, offer risk-reward advantages similar to the example above. The institutions who purchase them insist on such advantages to compensate for the expected poor trading liquidity later on. Individual investors can buy undervalued new issues without being burdened later by the problem of trading huge position sizes. However, smaller investors can gain even greater benefits by searching out bargains created by institutional selling in the secondary trading markets.

THE SECONDARY TRADING MARKET FOR CONVERTIBLE BONDS

The aftermarket liquidity problem is real for large holders of convertible bond positions, since the public is not actively involved in this market niche. Other

Table 4-2. Risk-reward analysis for XYZ Corp. convertible bond

Stock price in 12 months	10	20	40
Estimated convertible bond price	78	100	160
Common stock gain or (loss)	– 50%	0%	+100%
Convertible gain or (loss)	– 22%	0%	+ 60%
plus interest received	+ 10	+ 10	+ 10
total return	– 12%	+ 10%	+ 70%

Exhibit 4-2. The convertible price curve
XYZ Corp. 10 percent, 20-year bond trading at 90
- conversion ratio = 40 shares
- straight bond equivalent yield = 16 percent

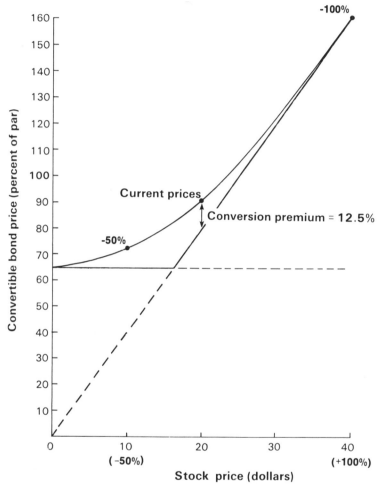

institutional investors routinely stay away from the convertible market simply because they wish to avoid trading problems should they later choose to sell. Thus, the number of available buyers, large and small, is far smaller than for most common stocks. When a large institutional holder does decide to sell, it hopes that another institution is willing to buy at a price reasonably close to the current market price. If a swap cannot be arranged, the price must be lowered to attract potential buyers.

Let's assume that the XYZ Corporation convertible's price is reduced to 90 with its common stock still at $20. As shown by Exhibit 4-2, the ten point

Table 4-3. Risk-reward analysis for XYZ Corp. convertible bond trading at 90

Stock price in 12 months	10	20	40
Estimated convertible bond price	72	90	160
Common stock gain or (loss)	– 50%	0%	+100%
Convertible gain or (loss)	– 20%	0%	+ 78%
plus interest received	+ 11	+ 11	+ 11
total return	– 9%	+ 11%	+ 89%

reduction cuts the conversion premium in half to only 12.5 percent. The lower convertible curve of Exhibit 4-2 passes through the new price of 90 and assumes the bond will remain on a lower price track over the near term. For instance, a stock price decline to $10 would now find the convertible trading at only 72, as compared to 78 in our previous example.

Table 4-3 presents risk-reward calculations for the bond at 90. Notice the improvements over the prior calculations at 100. Not only is current income increased from 10 to 11 percent and risk reduced further, but the convertible now offers nearly the full upside potential of its common stock—89 percent versus 100 percent over the next twelve months. If we add another year's 11 percent interest, the bond's total return of 100 percent will equal a stock doubling over a two-year period, while theoretically eliminating downside risk.

The XYZ Corporation convertible bond at 90 is substantially undervalued relative to its common stock. Note I am not passing judgment on the merits of the common stock itself; I assume the market has priced it efficiently. My only concern at the time the risk-reward calculations are made is the relationships between the two securities. Whether or not I want to own any securities of XYZ Corporation is a separate decision. However, if given such an undervalued opportunity, I would find some way to include the bond in my portfolio via a hedging strategy even if I didn't like the company. This is what convertible hedging is all about—taking advantage of undervalued opportunities in a low-risk investment posture.

A SAMPLE PORTFOLIO OF AGGRESSIVE CONVERTIBLE BONDS

Table 4-4 presents a ten-issue sample portfolio of aggressive convertible bonds available in early 1985 following the explosive January rally. Excluding, for a

Table 4-4. Undervalued aggressive convertible bonds available in February 1985

Company name	Bond description	Bond price	Current yield	Leverage* −50%	Leverage* +100%	Stock Volatility†
Anacomp	10.00–95	80	12.5%	−24%	+88%	170
Andersen Group	10.50–02	102	10.3	−20	+67	140
Data-Design Labs	12.25–00	122	9.9	−25	+93	125
Delmed	10.50–97	80	13.1	−25	+81	195
MGM Grand Hotels	9.50–00	92	10.2	−18	+73	130
Mobile Communications	11.00–04	123	8.9	−28	+88	165
Pan American	15.00–98	105	14.2	−11	+51	145
Recognition Equipment	11.00–06	114	9.6	−24	+76	175
Southwest Forest	10.00–03	106	9.4	−23	+74	135
Western Air Lines	14.00–98	108	13.0	−22	+75	180
Averages (10 positions)			11.1%	−22%	+77%	156

* The estimated percent change for the convertible for changes in the price of the underlying stock of −50 or +100 percent.

†Volatility is a measurement of a stock's past price fluctuations compared to the average stock having a 100 volatility.

Source: Noddings, Calamos & Associates' research.

moment, its yield advantage, the sample portfolio offered more than three-fourths the potential (+77 percent versus +100 percent) at less than half the risk (−22 percent versus −50 percent) of the underlying common stocks. Since the stocks paid little or no dividends, nearly all the convertible portfolio's 11.1 percent current yield will add to its potential, and reduce its risk, in a total-return comparison. The resulting portfolio total-return numbers of −11 percent and +88 percent are similar to the XYZ Corporation example when the bond was substantially undervalued at 90.

It's obvious from the sample portfolio that, even though seven of the ten underlying common stocks are New York Stock Exchange listed, they are not the kind of convertible bonds institutional money managers buy for their conservative clients. Therefore, institutional investors ignore this particular sector of the convertible securities market even more than they avoid the high-quality issues. Careful research will uncover the bargains in the low-quality (or low-capitalization, if you prefer) market sectors, and sophisticated hedging strategies can produce conservative portfolios using such speculative convertibles.

Chapter 5 will document historical performance data for both low-risk and aggressive convertibles. It will show that aftermarket bargains have been continually available, permitting real-world performance far exceeding their higher-risk common stock counterparts.

Historical-Performance Data for Undervalued Convertibles

Any superior investment strategy must be built on a logical foundation. The convertible securities market offers ideal tools for developing commonsense strategies, because each issue can be evaluated mathematically. Even when we assume efficiently priced underlying common stocks, portfolios of carefully selected convertibles can offer significant advantages over traditional stock portfolios.

THE CONVERTIBLE FUNDS

A superior strategy should also be verifiable by proven track records. I use the word *should* instead of *must* since some attractive strategies, having no performance history, do come along from time to time. However, they are usually exploited rather quickly by sophisticated professionals who do not insist on a prior track record and can therefore move promptly once an unusual opportunity is discovered. Fortunately, for those desiring proven performance before stepping in, there have long been pricing inefficiencies in the convertible securities markets. Seven professional convertible fund managers, with experience ranging up to more than twenty years, have made performance data available for inspection.

The seven funds include three closed-end (American Capital Fund, Bancroft Convertible Fund, and Castle Convertible Fund) and four mutual funds (American Capital Harbor Fund, Convertible Yield Securities, Phoenix Convertible Fund, and Putnam Convertible Fund). Their aggregate performance for the eleven years beginning with the bear-market year, 1974, compared with the S&P 500, as follows:

Year	Funds	S&P 500	Year	Funds	S&P 500
1974	− 11.8%	− 26.1%			
1975	+ 27.8	+ 36.6	1980	+ 30.8	+ 32.3
1976	+ 32.2	+ 24.2	1981	+ 3.9	− 4.9
1977	+ 4.6	− 7.4	1982	+ 27.4	+ 21.5
1978	+ 7.7	+ 6.8	1983	+ 19.3	+ 22.5
1979	+ 20.5	+ 18.4	1984	+ 1.6	+ 6.1

Source: A study conducted by Paul Heer, Vice President at Nashville's Third National Bank, as reported in Drexel Burnham Lambert's *The Convertible Letter,* February 1985.

The convertible funds outperformed the higher-risk Standard & Poor's 500 stock index by nearly four percentage points per year on average (14.1 percent annualized return for the eleven years versus 10.2 percent). Considering their management fees and trading expenses, compared to no expense calculated in the index, it is a feat that few conservative stock or fixed-income funds have accomplished (most high-performing funds invest in speculative stocks and thereby incur much greater risk). Appendix E lists each of the convertible funds plus two no-loads recently introduced by Noddings-Calamos Asset Management. You may call or write them for a no-obligation copy of their prospectus (load and no-load mutual funds) or annual report (closed-end funds).

It is also revealing to compare the seven convertible funds with the five option income funds of Chapter 2, since both groups involve stock market-related securities and have risk postures below that of the market. Over the past 7.5 years, since start-up of the option writing funds in mid-1977, the unheralded convertible funds returned 180 percent compared to only 102 percent for the heavily promoted option funds.

CONVERTIBLE BOND INDEXES

In addition to the performance records of the public funds, my firm maintains two convertible indexes based on actual trades made for our largest clients beginning in 1976. Unlike the convertible funds, which have different management styles that may change from time to time, our indexes split the convertible securities market into two distinctly different categories, low-risk and aggressive (Chapter 4). Hence, our indexes are more useful than the funds for analyzing opportunities in different market sectors and for the SuperHedging strategies to be introduced later.

I first presented the background for the indexes in my book, *The Investor's Guide to Convertible Bonds* (Dow Jones-Irwin, 1982). The material was expanded in my more recent book, *Low Risk Strategies for the High Performance Investor* (Probus Publishing, 1985). For those wanting specific information on how the indexes were constructed and maintained, refer to *Low Risk Strategies.* This chapter provides updated performance data in order to reconfirm that investing in undervalued convertibles does work and to develop the necessary groundwork for the superhedging strategies you will soon learn about.

THE NODDINGS-CALAMOS LOW-RISK CONVERTIBLE BOND INDEX

Table 5-1 shows the securities held in the low-risk index at year-end 1984. In accordance with our selection criteria, each of the convertible's underlying common stocks was ranked B+ or higher by Standard & Poor's and was New York Stock Exchange-listed. The index contained twenty-six issues and provided an average yield of 9.1 percent.

Table 5-2 presents quarterly total returns for the convertible index since its inception in 1976, compared with appropriate market standards: Standard & Poor's 500 stock index and the Salomon Brothers high-grade corporate bond index. Annual performance data for the three are provided in Table 5-3 along with statistical measurements of risk and return for five- and nine-year periods

Table 5-1. The Noddings-Calamos low-risk convertible bond index—positions held on December 31, 1984

Company name	Bond description	Bond price	Current yield	Stock beta	S&P stock rank
Allied Corp.[1]	7.75 −05	96.25	8.1%	1.15	A−
Allied Stores	8.75 −09	106.50	8.2	.80	A+
Celanese Corp.	9.75 −06	119.00	8.2	.90	B+
Chase Manhattan	6.50 −96	83.50	7.8	.95	A−
Data-Design Labs	12.25 −00	109.00	11.2	1.25	B+
GTE Corp.	10.50 −07	105.50	10.0	.90	A+
Inexco Oil	8.50 −00	58.25	14.6	1.40	B+
Kaneb Services[2]	8.75 −08	72.00	12.2	1.15	A−
Leggett & Platt	8.125−01	102.00	8.0	.90	A−
McKesson Corp.	9.75 −06	100.38	9.7	.75	A
Merrill Lynch	8.875−07	106.50	8.3	1.85	B+
Nat'l. Convenience Stores	9.00 −08	98.75	9.1	1.10	A−
Nat'l. Medical Enterprises	9.00 −06	110.12	8.2	1.40	A
Newell Cos.	8.75 −03	88.00	9.9	.85	A−
Nortek	10.50 −04	103.00	10.2	1.00	B+
Paine Webber[3]	8.00 −05	86.50	9.2	2.00	B+
Pogo Producing	8.00 −05	62.50	12.8	1.10	B+
Quaker State Oil	8.875−08	101.00	8.8	1.20	B+
Reynolds Industries[4]	10.00 −08	125.00	8.0	.90	A+
SCOA Industries	10.00 −07	116.00	8.6	.85	A+
Seagram Co. Ltd.	8.25 −08	115.00	7.2	1.05	A
Southwest Airlines	10.00 −07	128.00	7.8	1.15	B+
United Telecommun.[5]	5.00 −93	78.00	6.4	.90	A
Viacom International	9.25 −07	112.00	8.3	1.30	B+
Walter (Jim), Corp.	5.75 −91	96.75	5.9	1.15	B+
Westinghouse	9.00 −09	105.50	8.5	1.25	A+
Averages (26 positions)			9.1%	1.12	

[1] Bond trades as Textron
[2] Bond trades as Moran Energy
[3] Bond trades as CIGNA Corp.
[4] Bond trades as General Cinema
[5] Bond trades as United Utilities

Table 5-2. Quarterly returns for the Noddings-Calamos low-risk convertible bond index compared to appropriate market indexes—1976–84

Year	Quarter	Salomon Brothers bond index	S&P 500	Low-risk convertible bond index
1976	1	+ 4.2%	+ 15.0%	+ 18.0%
	2	+ 0.3	+ 2.4	+ 4.9
	3	+ 5.6	+ 1.9	+ 5.5
	4	+ 7.5	+ 3.1	+ 6.1
1977	1	− 2.3	− 7.5	− 1.4
	2	+ 3.9	+ 3.2	+ 6.2
	3	+ 1.1	− 2.8	− 1.3
	4	− 0.8	− 0.3	+ 1.4
1978	1	0.0	− 4.9	+ 2.4
	2	− 1.1	+ 8.5	+ 11.1
	3	+ 3.1	+ 8.7	+ 8.1
	4	− 2.0	− 5.0	− 9.8
1979	1	+ 1.6	+ 7.1	+ 9.3
	2	+ 4.5	+ 2.7	+ 6.8
	3	− 2.0	+ 7.6	+ 6.0
	4	− 7.9	+ 0.1	− 3.1
1980	1	− 13.5	− 4.1	− 6.5
	2	+ 25.1	+ 13.5	+ 20.7
	3	− 11.1	+ 11.2	+ 14.2
	4	+ 1.2	+ 9.5	+ 0.2
1981	1	− 1.1	+ 1.4	+ 7.6
	2	− 2.2	− 2.3	+ 4.8
	3	− 9.3	− 10.3	− 9.9
	4	+ 12.9	+ 6.9	+ 10.9
1982	1	+ 3.6	− 7.3	− 5.7
	2	+ 2.5	− 0.6	− 3.4
	3	+ 21.4	+ 11.5	+ 11.6
	4	+ 11.5	+ 18.2	+ 12.9
1983	1	+ 3.7	+ 10.0	+ 13.0
	2	+ 1.3	+ 11.1	+ 12.2
	3	− 0.3	− 0.2	− 1.6
	4	− 0.1	+ 0.4	− 2.2
1984	1	− 1.4	− 2.4	− 1.4
	2	− 4.6	− 2.6	− 1.5
	3	+ 13.4	+ 9.7	+ 6.6
	4	+ 9.1	+ 1.8	+ 2.2

Table 5-3. Annual returns for the Noddings-Calamos low-risk convertible bond index compared to appropriate market indexes—1976–84

Year	Salomon Brothers bond index	S&P 500	Low-risk convertible bond index
1976	+ 18.6%	+ 23.6%	+ 38.6%
1977	+ 1.7	− 7.2	+ 4.8
1978	− 0.1	+ 6.6	+ 10.9
1979	− 4.2	+ 18.4	+ 19.9
1980	− 2.6	+ 32.5	+ 29.1
1981	− 1.0	− 5.0	+ 12.7
1982	+ 43.7	+ 21.6	+ 14.8
1983	+ 4.7	+ 22.5	+ 22.0
1984	+ 16.4	+ 6.2	+ 5.8
5-year data			
Cumulative return	69%	99%	116%
Annualized return	11.1	14.8	16.7
Average quarterly return	3.1	3.8	4.2
Standard deviation	10.0	7.8	8.4
Coefficient of variation	323	205	198
9-year data			
Cumulative return	95%	188%	316%
Annualized return	7.7	12.5	17.2
Average quarterly return	2.2	3.2	4.3
Standard deviation	7.9	6.9	7.5
Coeffficient of variation	366	216	174

through 1984. The quarterly returns, plotted by Exhibit 5-1, indicate a high correlation between low-risk convertible bonds and the S&P 500, as would be expected, but a poor correlation with straight corporate bonds.

As Table 5-3 reveals, low-risk convertibles were profitable in each of the nine years versus seven positive years for the S&P 500 and five for straight bonds. The convertible index's five-year cumulative return was 116 percent as compared with 99 percent for common stocks and 69 percent for straight bonds. Its nine-year cumulative return was 316 percent versus 188 percent for stocks and only 95 percent for straight bonds. The 316 percent return also compared favorably with 280 percent appreciation experienced by the seven convertible funds over the same nine-year period.

Exhibit 5-1. The Noddings-Calamos low-risk convertible bond index versus appropriate market indexes—total returns, 1976–84.

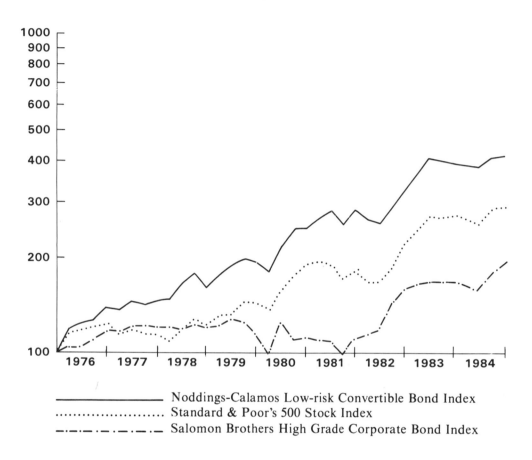

——————————— Noddings-Calamos Low-risk Convertible Bond Index
.... Standard & Poor's 500 Stock Index
—.—.—.—.—.— Salomon Brothers High Grade Corporate Bond Index

THE NODDINGS-CALAMOS AGGRESSIVE CONVERTIBLE BOND INDEX

Table 5-4 presents the year-end 1984 listing of the issues included in our aggressive convertible bond index. Of the twenty-five underlying common stocks, nine were listed on the New York Stock Exchange, six on the American, and ten were traded in the over-the-counter market. The convertible portfolio, with individual yields ranging from 7.3 to 22 percent, averaged 12.8 percent. This was higher than would be expected for someone setting up a new portfolio at the time, because I chose to hold several issues that had dropped to deeply

Table 5-4. The Noddings-Calamos agressive convertible bond index—positions held on December 31, 1984

Company name	Bond description		Bond price	Current yield	Vola-tility	S&P stock rank
American Adventure	10.00	–98	95.00	10.5%	175	NR
American Century Corp	6.75	–91	66.00	10.2	135	NR
American Maize Products	11.75	–00	104.50	11.2	120	B
Anacomp	10.00	–95	55.00	18.2	170	B–
Andersen Group	10.50	–02	88.00	11.9	140	B+
Beefsteak Charlies	13.00	–97	59.50	21.8	210	B–
Carl Karcher Enterprises	9.50	–07	95.50	9.9	130	NR
Computer Consoles	7.75	–98	73.50	10.5	155	B
Comserv Corp.	11.00	–02	51.00	21.6	230	B
Crime Control	10.00	–97	45.50	22.0	220	NR
Crystal Oil	11.375	–00	58.00	19.6	160	C
Delmed	10.50	–97	55.00	19.1	195	NR
Graphic Scanning	10.00	–01	73.00	13.7	155	C
Inter-Regional Financial	10.00	–03	78.00	14.7	130	B
Jerrico	8.50	–08	84.50	10.1	110	B+
MGM Grand Hotels	9.50	–00	84.00	11.3	130	NR
Mobile Communications	12.00	–02	131.00	9.2	150	NR
Pan American	15.00	–98	105.25	14.3	145	C
Pulte Home	8.50	–08	93.25	9.1	150	B
Recognition Equipment	11.00	–06	107.00	10.3	175	B–
Southwest Forest Industries	10.00	–03	105.00	9.5	135	C
Telepictures	10.00	–02	117.50	8.5	140	NR
US Air Group	9.25	–07	127.50	7.3	125	B
Walker Telecommunications	11.00	–99	140.00	7.9	175	NR
Western Air Lines	5.25	–93	63.00	8.3	150	C
Averages (25 positions)				12.8%	156	

discounted levels during the 1983-84 market decline of secondary stocks. A new portfolio of bonds trading near par should average about 11 percent as in Table 4-4 of Chapter 4.

Table 5-5 provides quarterly total returns for the convertible index, compared with the S&P 500 and the American Stock Exchange Index (AMEX). The riskiness of the convertible index's underlying common stocks probably falls somewhere between these extreme market evaluation standards. The quarterly

Table 5-5. Quarterly returns for the Noddings-Calamos aggressive convertible bond index compared to appropriate market indexes—1976-84

Year	Quarter	AMEX index	S&P 500	Aggressive convertible bond index
1976	1	+ 24.9%	+ 15.0%	+ 9.7%
	2	+ 1.0	+ 2.4	+ 9.0
	3	− 3.2	+ 1.9	+ 6.1
	4	+ 7.7	+ 3.1	+ 4.9
1977	1	+ 1.2	− 7.5	+ 1.5
	2	+ 8.2	+ 3.2	+ 4.9
	3	− 1.2	− 2.8	+ 0.5
	4	+ 7.6	− 0.3	+ 1.9
1978	1	+ 0.8	− 4.9	+ 10.6
	2	+ 12.9	+ 8.5	+ 10.4
	3	+ 16.0	+ 8.7	+ 14.7
	4	− 10.8	− 5.0	− 6.9
1979	1	+ 19.4	+ 7.1	+ 13.9
	2	+ 11.7	+ 2.7	+ 8.4
	3	+ 2.2	+ 7.6	+ 8.5
	4	+ 20.4	+ 0.1	+ 2.1
1980	1	− 5.7	− 4.1	− 4.2
	2	+ 26.0	+ 13.5	+ 15.7
	3	+ 12.9	+ 11.2	+ 11.2
	4	+ 5.3	+ 9.5	+ 7.2
1981	1	+ 3.3	+ 1.4	+ 11.8
	2	+ 3.9	− 2.3	+ 1.5
	3	− 21.8	− 10.3	− 12.1
	4	+ 9.5	+ 6.9	+ 4.7
1982	1	− 18.9	− 7.3	− 0.3
	2	− 3.6	− 0.6	+ 2.2
	3	+ 12.9	+ 11.5	+ 8.8
	4	+ 20.3	+ 18.2	+ 18.0
1983	1	+ 14.2	+ 10.0	+ 12.3
	2	+ 24.6	+ 11.1	+ 20.0
	3	− 5.0	− 0.2	− 7.6
	4	− 3.1	+ 0.4	− 1.4
1984	1	− 5.4	− 2.4	+ 1.2
	2	− 5.1	− 2.6	− 7.2
	3	+ 7.6	+ 9.7	+ 4.2
	4	− 5.2	+ 1.8	+ 1.1

Table 5-6. Annual returns for the Noddings-Calamos aggressive convertible bond index compared to appropriate market indexes—1976–84

Year	AMEX index	S&P 500	Aggressive convertible bond index
1976	+ 31.6%	+ 23.6%	+ 33.1%
1977	+ 16.4	− 7.2	+ 9.0
1978	+ 17.7	+ 6.6	+ 30.4
1979	+ 64.1	+ 18.4	+ 36.8
1980	+ 41.2	+ 32.5	+ 32.1
1981	− 8.1	− 5.0	+ 4.4
1982	+ 6.2	+ 21.6	+ 30.8
1983	+ 31.0	+ 22.5	+ 22.8
1984	− 8.4	+ 6.2	− 1.1
5-year data			
Cumulative return	65%	99%	119%
Annualized return	10.5	14.8	17.0
Average quarterly return	3.3	3.8	4.4
Standard deviation	13.0	7.8	8.8
Coefficient of variation	389	205	201
9-year data			
Cumulative return	389%	188%	467%
Annualized return	19.3	12.5	21.3
Average quarterly return	5.1	3.2	5.2
Standard deviation	11.7	7.0	7.5
Coefficient of variation	226	216	144

returns are plotted in Exhibit 5-2. Note that the aggressive convertible bond index kept pace with the high-performance AMEX, but quarterly price movements correlated better with the high-quality S&P 500. This observation was confirmed by stastistical analysis.

Table 5-6 shows annual performance data for the three indexes plus statistical measurements of risk and return. Aggressive convertibles experienced only one losing year during the past nine, a modest 1.1 percent loss in 1984. The AMEX and S&P 500 each had two negative years, ranging from −5.0 to −8.4 percent. The convertible's 9-year return of 467 percent produced a compounded rate in excess of 20 percent annually without incurring the high risk associated with speculative common stocks.

Exhibit 5-2. The Noddings-Calamos aggressive convertible bond index versus appropriate market indexes—total returns, 1976-84.

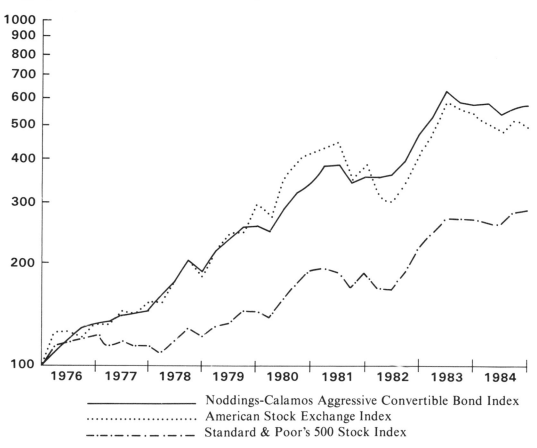

_____ Noddings-Calamos Aggressive Convertible Bond Index
.... American Stock Exchange Index
_.._.._.._.._ Standard & Poor's 500 Stock Index

RISK-REWARD ANALYSIS

I have found risk to be one of the most difficult subjects to discuss with investors. Everyone seems to have his own definition, and these definitions may vary from one investment vehicle to another. For example, many investors view stock market risk as the possibility of losing money over the near term, and often become discouraged when prices decline. At the same time, they may be comfortable holding long-term bonds, even though current prices may be well below their costs.

Market scholars analyze risk through statistical calculations. The *variability of return,* a measurement of a portfolio's fluctuating market value, as described by its standard deviation, is commonly employed by professional investors. Unfortunately, the standard deviation falls short of perfection when comparing risks for different investment strategies. For instance, a highly profitable strategy might be very volatile, hence a high standard deviation, but never lose money. Would it be considered risky? If so, why?

One possible improvement over the standard deviation's weakness is to express it as a percentage of the mean. This produces the *coefficient of variation,* a risk measurement which adjusts for the fact that a larger standard deviation is to be expected when the mean is higher. For reference, the formula is:

$$V = \frac{\sigma}{\overline{x}} \times 100$$

where   V = coefficient of variation
          σ = standard deviation
          $\overline{x}$ = mean (e.g. average quarterly return)

Tables 5-3 and 5-6 include both standard deviation and coefficient of variation calculations for each of the strategies discussed. Time periods cover both the past five years and nine years (the life of the two convertible bond indexes). The five-year data, showing annualized returns on the vertical axis and quarterly coefficients of variation on the horizontal axis, are plotted in Exhibit 5-3. The nine-year data are plotted in Exhibit 5-4. Each graph includes a straight line connecting Treasury bills and the S&P 500—the capital market line presented in the Introduction. The capital market line is the industry standard against which all other investment strategies may be compared; above-the-line performance is every investor's goal.

From the exhibits, note how poorly straight bonds have done during both the five- and nine-year periods. Not only have they underperformed the stock and money markets, they have done so at a much higher level of risk. Speculative stocks would be expected to outperform high-quality stocks, and this was certainly true for the AMEX index over the longer term. However, the AMEX underperformed during the past five years. The only consistent winners were convertible bonds, both low-risk and aggressive. They provided above-the-line performance for both time periods, at risk levels below those of traditional stocks and bonds.

Exhibit 5-3. Risk-reward analysis for selected indexes, 5 years (1980–84)

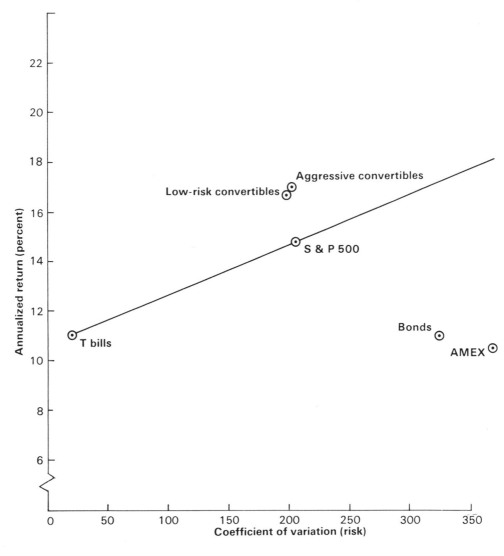

ARE AGGRESSIVE CONVERTIBLES RISKY?

The risk-reward data for the aggressive convertible bond index have particular significance. As Table 5-6 reveals, the aggressive index experienced higher standard deviations than the S&P 500 for both the five- and nine-year periods, indicating greater risk by normal standards. However, its coefficients of variation

Exhibit 5-4. Risk-reward analysis for selected indexes, 9 years (1976–1984)

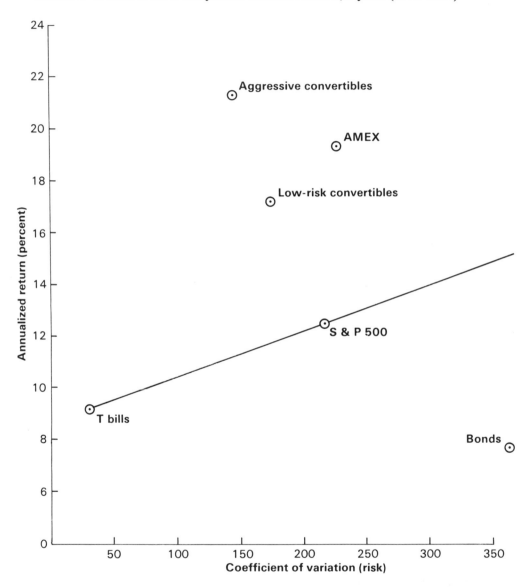

were lower than the S&P, especially over the longer term. The advantages of investing in these more speculative securities are highlighted by the plots of Exhibit 5-4. Here, their risk level was about the same as a combination portfolio of T-bills and stocks, but their annualized return was nearly twice as great, 21.3 percent versus 10.8 percent.

Some might conclude that the convertible bond market is becoming less attractive, because 1984 was a losing year for the aggressive index (−1.1 percent), whereas the S&P 500 earned 6.2 percent. Having first-hand knowledge of the bonds making up the index during 1984, however, I can advise that this was a year of negative divergence. The common stocks underlying the convertibles performed well below average for the twelve months; this situation reversed itself during the early months of 1985. For the first half, the aggressive convertible index outperformed the market averages. Updated performance figures are as follows:

	1st Half '85	*9.5 years*
Aggressive convertibles	+ 19.0%	+ 575%
AMEX index	+ 13.1	+ 453
Standard & Poor's 500 index	+ 17.2	+ 238

Any portfolio of around twenty-five securities will underperform broad-based market indexes from time to time. This is to be expected; it's a risk experienced by all investors, both individuals and professionals. Over the longer term, however, divergences should average out and portfolios of carefully selected convertibles should provide higher returns, as anticipated. Remember, investing is a long-term activity; short-term fluctuations have little or no significance when seeking long-term results.

CHAPTER 6

Hedging Convertible Bonds with Common Stock

Convertible-bond hedging permits conservative investors to take advantage of undervalued opportunities, regardless of how speculative they may be. By selling common stock short against carefully selected convertibles, the conservative investor can retain much of the stock market's potential while eliminating most of the investment risk.

Although any undervalued convertible may be hedged by shorting stock, the strategy is best suited for the more aggressive issues. They tend to be more undervalued than higher-quality convertibles; their yields are usually greater; and because their underlying stocks pay little or no dividends, the payment of the short sale dividend is not a serious burden. Thus, the ideal convertible hedge candidate is a high-yielding bond trading at its conversion value, with a volatile underlying common stock paying no dividend. While the ideal candidate can be found on occasion, we must usually accept compromises on these selection parameters. Let's evaluate a typical attractive situation.

CONVERTIBLE/STOCK HEDGING

Chapter 4 illustrated the risk-reward characteristics for an XYZ Corporation 10 percent convertible bond brought to the market at 100. It showed how trading in the aftermarket might result in a price drop to 90, at which point the bond would be significantly undervalued. At a price of 90, the XYZ convertible would be a hedge candidate. Normally, hedging opportunities can be found after price advances.

Let's assume, for example, that XYZ common stock advances from $20 up to $30 shortly after the convertible was issued. At a $30 stock price, the convertible is worth 120 if exchanged for common (40 shares × $30 per share = $1,200). Assuming that the convertible was not callable for another year or so, its normal price should be near 130, but suppose it could be purchased for only 122, as shown by Exhibit 6-1.

At 122, though mathematically undervalued, the convertible would probably be considered too risky for most conservative investors—XYZ Corporation is still a speculative company, and the bond is trading at nearly twice its $650 investment floor. In fact, that might be why those who purchased the bond at 100 are selling at 122. Sellers may be perfectly satisfied with a 22 percent capital gain in addition to the 10 percent coupon; they may be seeking the safety of a replacement issue at 100. Other conservative investors, who have the ability to execute hedging strategies (most institutions are legally prevented from shorting stock), can take advantage of such an attractive opportunity via the convertible/stock hedge.

THE BULLISH HEDGE

The risk-reward calculations and profit profile of Exhibit 6-2 illustrate a bullish hedge position. For this, and the neutral and bearish positions to follow, I made these assumptions:

- Ten bonds are purchased at 122 for a cash investment of $12,200 (margin will be evaluated separately).
- The common stock at $30 pays a 2 percent annual dividend, or $15 each quarter per 100 shares—short sellers must pay the dividend to the stock lender.

Exhibit 6-1. Convertible price curve for XYZ Corp. 10 percent, 20-year bond trading at 122 with the common stock at 30
- conversion ratio = 40 shares
- straight bond equivalent yield = 16 percent

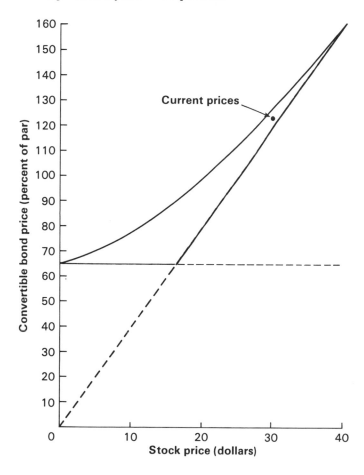

- Short sale proceeds are credited to a special short account and held by the brokerage firm until the stock is later bought back. These funds are frozen and are not available for use by the short seller.
- Risk-reward calculations are based on a six-month holding period. Whereas most hedge positions are held longer, six months permits a direct comparison with the option strategies of Chapter 1 and those to be presented in Chapter 7.
- Commissions are again excluded for ease of illustration.

Exhibit 6-2. Convertible bonds hedged by the short sale of stock—bullish posture

	Price	*Prices in Six Months*			
Stock	$ 30.00	$ 15	$ 30	$ 45	$ 60
Convertible	122.00	85	122	180	240

Strategy 19: Buy 10 bonds and short 200 shares of stock ($6000)*

Profit or (loss) on bonds	(3700)	0	5800	11800
Profit or (loss) on stock	3000	0	(3000)	(6000)
Bond interest received	500	500	500	500
Stock dividends paid	(60)	(60)	(60)	(60)
Total profit or (loss)	(260)	440	3240	6240
Return on investment	− 2.1%	+ 3.6%	+ 26.6%	+ 51.1%
Annualized return	− 4.2%	+ 7.2%	+ 53.2%	+ 102.2%

*Investment = $1220 per bond X 10 bonds = $12200

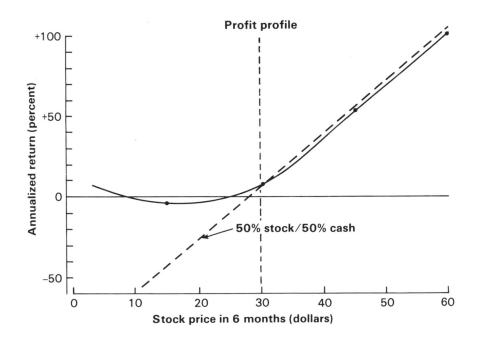

As shown by the risk-reward calculations of Exhibit 6-2, the bullish hedge assumes the short sale of 200 common shares. Since ten bonds represent 400 shares, this amounts to a half hedge and is designed to simply reduce downside risk. If the common were to drop in half to $15 over the ensuing six months, the $3,700 loss on the ten-bond position would be largely offset by the short sale's $3,000 profit plus the $440 net interest earned ($500 received for ten bonds minus $60 in stock dividends paid). The six-month total loss of $260 equals −2.1 percent on the $12,200 investment, or −4.2 percent annualized. If the 50 percent stock decline happened more quickly, the loss would be greater; if it took longer than six months, the additional interest earned would ultimately produce downside profits.

In a static market, the hedge position provides a net interest income of 7.2 percent annually, well above that of the typical common stock. The desired outcome, however, is for the stock to make a strong advance. Here, the bond profits would exceed short sale losses, providing significant capital appreciation. If the stock were to gain 50 percent to $45, for instance, the hedge's annualized return would be 53 percent; a stock doubling to $60 would produce a 102 percent annualized return.

Bullish hedges, as illustrated, are designed to participate in upward market movements at reduced risk. These hedges are excellent alternatives to holding blue chip common stocks outright. Since their underlying common stocks are more volatile than high quality stocks, diversified portfolios of such conservative hedges can do nearly as well during market advances as an index like the S&P 500, while minimizing losses during market declines. Over a market cycle, a convertible hedge program should do as well as or better than the higher-risk stock market.

NEUTRAL AND BEARISH HEDGES

For investors desiring greater safety than that provided by bullish hedging, or even downside profits, additional common shares can be shorted, up to 400 against a ten-bond position. Exhibit 6-3 presents a neutral hedge involving 300 shares short. Exhibit 6-4 shows a bearish hedge involving a full 400-share short position.

These more-bearish tactics are recommended to investors employing market timing who believe XYZ Corporation is about to experience a price decline. Technicians can quickly shift from a bullish to a bearish stance by adding to the

Exhibit 6-3. Convertible bonds hedged by the short sale of stock—neutral posture

	Price	*Prices in Six Months*			
Stock	$ 30.00	$ 15	$ 30	$ 45	$ 60
Convertible	122.00	85	122	180	240

Strategy 20: Buy 10 bonds and short 300 shares of stock ($9000)*

Profit or (loss) on bonds	(3700)	0	5800	11800
Profit or (loss) on stock	4500	0	(4500)	(9000)
Bond interest received	500	500	500	500
Stock dividends paid	(90)	(90)	(90)	(90)
Total profit or (loss)	1210	410	1710	3210
Return on investment	+ 9.9%	+ 3.4%	+14.0%	+26.3%
Annualized return	+19.8%	+ 6.8%	+28.0%	+52.6%

*Investment = $1220 per bond X 10 bonds = $12200

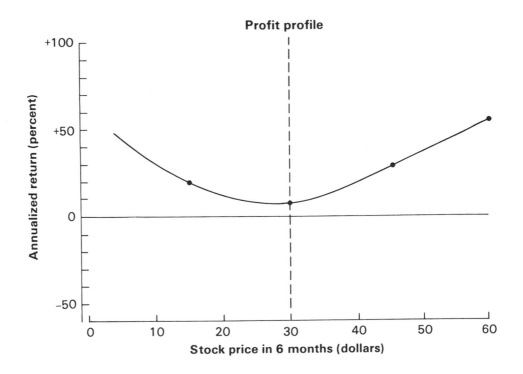

Profit profile

Exhibit 6-4. Convertible bonds hedged by the short sale of stock—bearish posture

	Price	*Prices in Six Months*			
Stock	$ 30.00	$ 15	$ 30	$ 45	$ 60
Convertible	122.00	85	122	180	240

Strategy 21: Buy 10 bonds and short 400 shares of stock ($12000)*

Profit or (loss) on bonds	(3700)	0	5800	11800
Profit or (loss) on stock	6000	0	(6000)	(12000)
Bond interest received	500	500	500	500
Stock dividends paid	(120)	(120)	(120)	(120)
Total profit or (loss)	2680	380	180	180
Return on investment	+22.0%	+ 3.1%	+ 1.5%	+ 1.5%
Annualized return	+44.0%	+ 6.2%	+ 3.0%	+ 3.0%

*Investment = $1220 per bond X 10 bonds = $12200

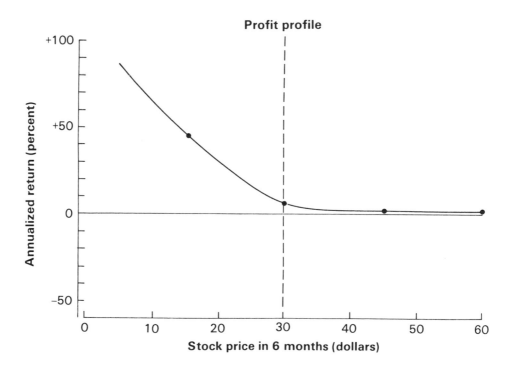

Profit profile

shares sold short without liquidating their entire positions and incurring large trading expenses. Nor is it necessary to terminate the holding period of their long securities, which might result in short-term capital gains instead of favorable long-term gains. When they turn bullish once again, they can simply cover a portion of the stock held short.

Hedgers who disregard short-term price movements should remain in a bullish posture throughout a market cycle. A bullish stance is not only more compatible with the stock market's long-term upward bias, it will produce greater profits during volatile sideways movements. The odds are roughly equal that a stock will either drop in half or double (if both were to happen during successive price movements, the stock would end up where it started). The bullish hedge offers much higher profits if the stock doubles than a bearish hedge does if the stock halves; the neutral hedge falls in between. Thus, investors lacking forecasting ability will reap greater profits over the long run by staying in a bullish posture. A rough way to measure the relative merits of different strategies is to multiply their values after a 100-percent stock advance by those after a 50-percent stock decline.

$$\text{Bullish hedge (Exhibit 6-2): } 2.022 \times 0.958 = 94\%$$
$$\text{Neutral hedge (Exhibit 6-3): } 1.526 \times 1.198 = 83\%$$
$$\text{Bearish hedge (Exhibit 6-4): } 1.030 \times 1.440 = 48\%$$

Investors who do not employ market timing, however, may also have use for neutral or bearish convertible hedges if they have unhedged convertibles in their portfolios. The net result can produce a low-risk posture for the total portfolio, as if each convertible security were individually protected. Convertibles and their related hedging strategies provide portfolio-management flexibility unavailable to investors using conventional stocks, bonds, and money market instruments.

CONSTRUCTING A CONVERTIBLE HEDGE PORTFOLIO

Two key elements—research and order execution—are the heart of a successful convertible hedge portfolio. Important in any investment program, they must be given extra attention when dealing with convertibles and related hedging strategies.

Research begins with a careful screening of the several hundred potential candidates. Of the total number available, perhaps fifty convertibles offering superior risk-reward characteristics will be targeted for detailed analysis—those issues having low conversion premiums, high yield advantages, and volatile underlying stocks.

Preparation of estimated convertible price curves and risk-reward calculations for each candidate are the next steps in the selection process. At this point, the list will probably narrow down to approximately fifteen semifinalists. Assuming that you wish to ultimately have a diversified portfolio of about twenty positions, the best ten or so should be put on initially and added to later as other candidates become equally attractive.

Next, the best way to enter orders must be determined, remembering that a hedge position involves two sides and that short sales may only be executed on an up-tick (an increase in price over the previous sale). Order execution decisions include whether to enter the long or short side first; whether to use market or limit orders; and, finally, how to execute the other side once the first order is filled. At times, during rapidly changing markets, filling both sides of a hedge near your target prices may not be possible. That is one of the risks you must accept when implementing a hedging program.

Since holding a naked short position in a rising market is an uncomfortable experience, most hedgers will purchase the convertible bond first, then short the stock later. The alternative is to attempt a simultaneous execution; however, this is a difficult transaction, because the securities trade in different markets and the bid price for the stock must be an up-tick. In addition, the bid-ask price spread for both sides of the trade is relinquished. Over the long run, this can be more costly than occasionally missing a target price.

MANAGING THE HEDGE PORTFOLIO

Hedging convertible bonds via the short sale of common stock can be a relatively passive investment strategy, since large price movements are usually necessary before action need be taken.

This strategy's ideal market environment is a bull market in secondary stocks such as the six-year period from the end of the 1974 bear market through 1980, and also from mid-1982 through mid-1983. Under such favorable conditions, profits are taken when bonds advance to well above par, and the funds are reinvested in new positions priced closer to par. Always maintaining the portfolio in a low-risk posture in preparation for the next market downturn is the hedger's objective.

While managing a convertible hedge portfolio during advancing markets is not too difficult, bear markets can present unforeseeable problems. Although bullishly constructed hedges, for example, are designed to break-even during bear markets, rising interest rates and/or panic sell-offs can push the bonds well below the theoretical investment floors assigned at the time they were originally purchased. Like economists who tend to forecast three out of every one business recessions, the market seems to predict far more corporate bankruptcies than actually occur. Thus, hedgers are sometimes faced with losing positions when the short sale profits cease to protect bonds driven to deeply discounted price levels. My advice is: Don't panic. Let's look at the bullish hedge in XYZ Corporation as an illustration of what one can expect to experience on occasion.

Originally established at prices of 122 and $30 for the XYZ Corporation bonds and stock, the hedge, involving 200 shares sold short against ten bonds, was intended to break-even on the downside when including interest earned (Exhibit 6-2). If the stock plummeted from $30 down to $5 over the next twelve months, as an extreme example, the ten bonds were expected to lose no more than $5,700 as they approached their $650 investment floor. In theory, this loss would have been more than offset by short sale profits of $5,000 plus $880 net interest earned. But suppose that the decline were accompanied by large corporate losses and rising fears that the company was headed into bankruptcy. In that event, the market might drop the convertible's price to well below 65. At a price of 40, for instance, a net position loss of $2,300 would exist, or nearly 20 percent on the original investment.

Studies have shown that deep-discount bonds, like XYZ Corporation at 40, significantly outperform the markets, on average.* Thus, it would make little sense to close out the entire position. Rather, I would normally cover the shorted stock for profits and hold the bond unhedged. At 40, its current yield is 25 percent, and the ten-bond position, worth only $4,000, now makes up but a small portion of the total portfolio, assuming a number of similar positions were taken. (Note that much of the original $12,200 investment was returned during the twelve-month decline through the process of marking the short account to the market.)

Recognize that some deep-discount bonds will experience further declines; others that recover should more than offset the additional losses of those that

---

*   *Low Risk Strategies for the High Performance Investor*, Chapter 6.

don't. In fact, the unhedged XYZ bond at 40 is probably no more risky, and potentially just as profitable, as the original hedge position. Hence, over time, a convertible hedge portfolio can be expected to include unhedged bonds trading at deep-discount levels up to hedged bonds trading above par. The twenty-five issues making up the Noddings-Calamos aggressive convertible bond index at the end of 1984 (Table 5-4), for example, all of which were previously hedged when trading near par, included six unhedged issues trading below 60 at the time.

HEDGING ON MARGIN

Convertible bond hedging is a superior strategy for both tax-exempt portfolios and tax-paying individuals. Although some tax-exempt investors may be prohibited from using margin, individuals should seriously consider the extra benefits obtainable through the use of leverage. Not only are portfolio returns expected to exceed the cost of borrowed money, thus providing leveraged profits, but margin interest paid also reduces taxable income. The anticipated result is that most portfolio appreciation will be favorably taxed as long-term capital gains.

Illustrated in the following exhibits are the risks and rewards of convertible hedging on margin for the previously discussed bullish, neutral, and bearish postures. Look first at Exhibit 6-5 which shows the bullish hedge involving 200 shares sold short against ten XYZ Corporation bonds. At 50 percent margin, the net investment is $6,100—the remaining $6,100 is borrowed from the brokerage firm, assuming an interest charge of 11 percent (1 percent above the 10 percent going rate for risk-free money). Note that the shorted stock, covered by the convertibles, requires no additional margin. The $340 margin interest charge for six months reduces the net interest earned from $440 down to $100, or 3.2 percent annually on the $6,100 investment. Downside risk is increased from −4.2 percent annualized to −19.6 percent, and upside opportunity from +102 percent to +193 percent.

Investors wishing to avoid the higher risk of a margined bullish hedge would short additional stock as shown by the neutral position of Exhibit 6-6. Here, the margin leverages both upside and downside profits while reducing the annual cash flow in a sideways market from 6.8 percent to 2.4 percent. The bear hedge of Exhibit 6-7 leverages downside profits and produces modest losses if the stock rises.

Exhibit 6-5. A bullish convertible bond hedge position on 50 percent margin

	Price	*Prices in Six Months*			
Stock	$ 30.00	$ 15	$ 30	$ 45	$ 60
Convertible	122.00	85	122	180	240

Strategy 22: Buy 10 bonds on margin and short 200 shares of stock*

Profit or (loss) on bonds		(3700)	0	5800	11800
Profit or (loss) on stock		3000	0	(3000)	(6000)
Bond interest received		500	500	500	500
Margin interest paid at 11%		(340)	(340)	(340)	(340)
Stock dividends paid		(60)	(60)	(60)	(60)
Total profit or (loss)		(600)	100	2900	5900
Return on investment		− 9.8%	+ 1.6%	+47.5%	+96.7%
Annualized return		−19.6%	+ 3.2%	+95.0%	+193.4%

*Investment = $1220 per bond × 10 bonds × 50% = $6100

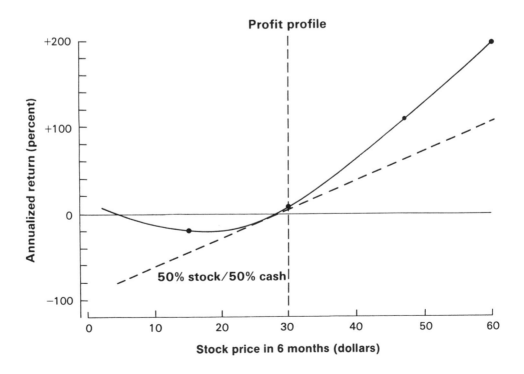

Profit profile

Exhibit 6-6. A neutral convertible bond hedge position on 50 percent margin

	Price	\$ 15	*Prices in Six Months*		
			\$ 30	\$ 45	\$ 60
Stock	\$ 30.00	\$ 15	\$ 30	\$ 45	\$ 60
Convertible	122.00	85	122	180	240

Strategy 23: Buy 10 bonds on margin and short 300 shares of stock*

Profit or (loss) on bonds	(3700)	0	5800	11800
Profit or (loss) on stock	4500	0	(4500)	(9000)
Bond interest received	500	500	500	500
Margin interest paid at 11%	(340)	(340)	(340)	(340)
Stock dividends paid	(90)	(90)	(90)	(90)
Total profit or (loss)	870	70	1370	2870
Return on investment	+ 14.3%	+ 1.2%	+ 22.5%	+ 47.0%
Annualized return	+ 28.6%	+ 2.4%	+ 45.0%	+ 94.0%

*Investment = $1220 per bond × 10 bonds × 50% = $6100

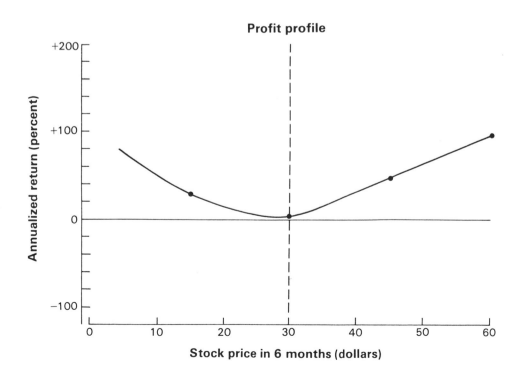

Profit profile

Exhibit 6-7. A bearish convertible bond hedge position on 50 percent margin

	Price	*Prices in Six Months*			
Stock	$ 30.00	$ 15	$ 30	$ 45	$ 60
Convertible	122.00	85	122	180	240

Strategy 24: Buy 10 bonds on margin and short 400 shares of stock*

Profit or (loss) on bonds	(3700)	0	5800	11800
Profit or (loss) on stock	6000	0	(6000)	(12000)
Bond interest received	500	500	500	500
Margin interest paid at 11%	(340)	(340)	(340)	(340)
Stock dividends paid	(120)	(120)	(120)	(120)
Total profit or (loss)	2340	40	(160)	(160)
Return on investment	+ 38.4%	+ 0.7%	- 2.6%	- 2.6%
Annualized return	+ 76.8%	+ 1.4%	- 5.2%	- 5.2%

*Investment = $1220 per bond × 10 bonds × 50% = $6100

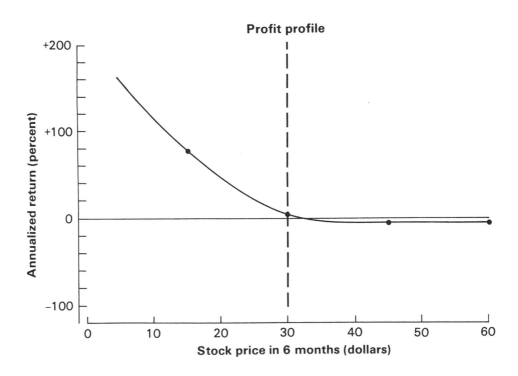

Profit profile

As shown by the examples, margin should increase the anticipated returns from a convertible hedge program in tandem with income tax savings—assuming that one's portfolio is carefully managed to assure that realized net capital gains are long term. Margin also provides an additional benefit to small investors: it permits them to increase their diversification by putting on more positions, which in turn reduces the risk of their overall portfolios.

CHAPTER 7

Hedging Convertible Bonds with Puts and Calls

Shorting stock was the primary strategy for protecting undervalued convertibles until the introduction of listed call options in 1973. This event opened the door to an ever-expanding grab bag of financial instruments useful in hedging market risk. Through the years, put options were added and the number of stocks with listed puts and calls has continually increased (see Appendix B for the 373 companies with listed options in April 1985). Since puts and calls offer additional portfolio-management flexibility and may be potentially more profitable than shorting stock, all convertible hedgers must be able to deal effectively with option strategies if they are to successfully compete. This chapter will show you how.

THE UNIVERSE OF CONVERTIBLES WITH LISTED OPTIONS

Selected convertibles should constitute the core holdings of any option-hedging program seeking above-average performance. Option hedging cannot be profitable unless the securities purchased are undervalued or the calls sold are overpriced. One of these conditions must exist or stockbrokers and market-makers will be the only winners. The option market, however, is reasonably efficient; thus, overpriced calls are scarce. We must turn to undervalued convertibles as the anchor of our option-hedging portfolios.

Of the 373 companies with listed puts and calls on their common stocks in April 1985, 136 also had convertible securities within their financial structure (Appendix C). A total of 204 different convertible bonds and convertible preferreds of these companies were trading at the time. Appendix C includes Standard & Poor's ranks of the underlying common stocks. Of the 136 companies, 90 were ranked B+ or higher, 42 were ranked below B+, and 4 were not ranked. Option strategists had a variety of both low-risk and aggressive convertible issues to consider in lieu of common stocks.

Table 7-1 presents a ten-issue sample portfolio of undervalued convertible bonds and preferreds chosen from Appendix C. All were trading at low conversion premiums, yielding above 6 percent, and providing a yield advantage over their underlying stocks. As shown in the leverage columns, these attractive convertible issues were targeted to keep pace with their underlying stocks upon a market advance, and were at less risk if the market fell. Informed option

Table 7-1. Undervalued convertible bonds and preferreds having listed options in April 1985

Company name	Convertible description	Convertible price	Current yield	Leverage* −50%	Leverage* +50%	Stock Volatil- ity†
Allied Stores	9.50 −07	139	6.8%	−30%	+50%	80
American Can	$ 3.00 pfd	46	6.5	−35	+50	80
Boeing Co.	8.875−06	142	6.3	−30	+50	100
Crown Zellerbach	$ 4.50 pfd	61	7.4	−25	+50	100
Deere & Co.	5.50 −01	90	6.1	−35	+50	90
Hercules	6.50 −99	100	6.5	−30	+45	95
ITT	$ 4.00 pfd	61	6.6	−30	+45	110
RCA	$ 2.125 pfd	31	6.9	−25	+45	90
Sybron	$ 2.40 pfd	32	7.6	−25	+45	90
Viacom International	9.25 −07	129	7.2	−30	+50	115

*The estimated percent change for the convertible for changes in the price of the underlying stock of −50 or +50 percent.

†Volatility is a measurement of a stock's past price fluctuations compared to the average stock having a 100 volatility.

Source: Noddings, Calamos & Associates' research

writers would have chosen them over the common stocks. Skilled hedgers seldom own stocks; they recognize that better alternatives exist in the convertible securities markets.

Let's now return to listed options to see portfolio-management opportunities available when combining them with undervalued convertibles.

PUTS AND CALLS VERSUS SHORTING STOCK

Basic option Strategy 4a (Chapter 1) illustrated how a simultaneous purchase of an at-the-money put and sale of an at-the-money call was analogous to selling stock short. Let's review the primary differences between the two tactics: the price spread between the put and call, kept in line through the conversion process, becomes a net credit to the account; short-sale dividends are not paid. In actuality, the long-put/short-call combination permits hedgers to capture the value of risk-free money whereas short-sale proceeds are frozen.

Portfolio-management flexibility is another advantage. Hedgers may select either the put or the call that fine tunes their portfolio's risk-reward characteristics and takes advantage of underpriced or overpriced opportunities. The price spread between the two options, for example, might properly reflect the value of money, yet both options may be undervalued or overvalued. If both are undervalued, one would hedge convertibles with long puts only—if both are overvalued, call writing would be the favored strategy.

Table 7-2. Various premium levels for put and call options on XYZ common stock trading at $30.00

	Option premium levels		
	Under-valued	Normally-valued	Over-valued
Call option premiums	7.50%	10.00%	12.50%
Put option premiums	3.75%	6.25%	8.75%
Call option price	$2.25	$3.00	$3.75
Put option price	$1.125	$1.875	$2.625
Price difference	$1.125	$1.125	$1.125

Table 7-2 analyzes six-month at-the-money puts and calls trading at various premium levels on XYZ stock selling at $30. The center column shows the same percentages used for the basic option strategies of Chapter 1: call and put premiums of 10 and 6.25 percent respectively. We can assume that a $3 call and a $1.875 put represent normal values since they are reasonably close to real-world premiums for options on typical stocks. The $1.125 price difference reflects risk-free money at 10 percent when XYZ stock yields 2 percent (Strategy 4a).

The outer columns of the table indicate possible prices, assuming both options are either underpriced or overpriced. Studying the undervalued options in the first column tells us that hedgers would buy puts trading at $1.125 and avoid selling calls at $2.25. From the overvalued options in the right-hand column, we know hedgers would sell calls at $3.75 and avoid buying puts at $2.625. The $.75 price differences from normal values means an extra 2.5 percent every six months—a 5 percent higher annual return than when dealing with normal option premiums.

Let's move on and evaluate various option-hedging strategies using the XYZ convertible bonds priced at 122, as in the convertible/stock hedging strategies of Chapter 6. The risk-reward calculations are based on these assumptions:

- Ten bonds are purchased at 122 for a cash investment of $12,200.
- The common stock is trading at $30.
- A normally valued six-month call option, having an exercise price of $30, is trading at $3.
- A normally valued six-month put option, also having a $30 strike price, is trading at $1.875.
- Each position is held until the options expire in six months.
- Options are assumed to be trading at their intrinsic values at expiration.
- Net premiums received from option transactions are placed in Treasury bills yielding 10 percent.
- Commissions are again excluded for ease of illustration.

HEDGING UNDERVALUED CONVERTIBLES WITH PUT OPTIONS

Ten XYZ convertible bonds are exchangeable into 400 shares of common stock. Thus, the purchase of four puts represents a full hedge position. Exhibit 7-1 provides the risk-reward calculations and profit profile. As shown, the puts not only protect the bonds in a declining market, the hedge begins to produce profits if the stock drops below $27.50. At a stock price of $15, for instance, a

Exhibit 7-1. Convertible bonds hedged by the purchase of put options

	Price	*Prices in Six Months*			
Stock	$ 30.00	$ 15	$ 30	$ 45	$ 60
Convertible	122.00	85	122	180	240
Put	1.875	15	0	0	0

Strategy 25: Buy 10 bonds and buy 4 at-the-money puts*

Profit or (loss) on bonds	(3700)	0	5800	11800
Profit or (loss) on puts	5250	(750)	(750)	(750)
Bond interest received	500	500	500	500
Interest charge on $750	(38)	(38)	(38)	(38)
Total profit or (loss)	2012	(288)	5512	11512
Return on investment	+16.5%	– 2.4%	+45.2%	+94.4%
Annualized return	+33.0%	– 4.8%	+90.4%	+188.8%

*Investment = $1220 per bond × 10 bonds = $12200

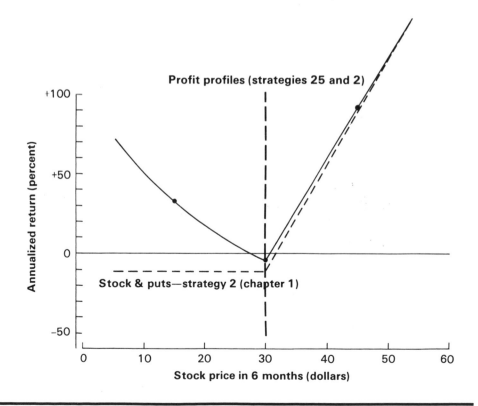

Profit profiles (strategies 25 and 2)

Stock & puts—strategy 2 (chapter 1)

Annualized return (percent)

Stock price in 6 months (dollars)

net six-month profit of 16.5 percent is anticipated. If the stock ends up unchanged at $30, the bond interest earned offsets most of the put-option acquisition costs; the net loss is 2.4 percent. Protecting convertibles with put options is a bullish strategy. If the stock were to double, the net profit would be 94 percent—the hoped-for outcome is for the stock to advance.

Exhibit 7-1 also includes the profit profile for protecting common stock with puts (Strategy 2 of Chapter 1). Once again, we can observe the advantages of dealing with undervalued convertible securities. Not only does the convertible/ put-option hedge offer downside profits, it will do as well, or better, as the stock/put combination upon a price advance. By overlooking the undervalued convertible bond, anyone purchasing XYZ common stock at the time made a serious investment error. Sadly, most investors are unaware that attractive convertibles might be available on stocks they are evaluating.

Bullish investors might reduce the number of normally valued puts purchased; they would recognize that hedging undervalued convertibles requires fewer puts than when protecting common stocks. If two puts were purchased to protect the ten-bond position, the six-month loss for a 50 percent stock price decline would be about 5 percent. The cost savings for purchasing only two puts increases the hedge-position returns in stable or rising markets.

HEDGING UNDERVALUED CONVERTIBLES WITH CALL OPTIONS

Exhibit 7-2 presents risk-reward calculations and the profit profile for writing covered call options against the ten XYZ convertible bonds. Like selling calls against common stocks, this low-risk strategy produces modest returns most of the time. However, by comparing the convertible hedge results with the stock position results, we can again recognize the advantages offered by undervalued securities. Not only does the convertible's higher yield provide additional profits in stable or rising markets, its investment floor cushions downside losses.

A popular tool for evaluating option-writing strategies is the break-even price—the common stock's price at which losses begin to accrue at the call's expiration. For the stock hedge, the break-even price is $26.50; for the convertible hedge, it is $24. More important than a lower break-even price is the fact that potential losses on the convertible hedge are much lower than on the stock position. For example, if the stock were to halve to $15, the convertible hedge would be expected to lose only 15.9 percent for the six-month period, compared to 38.5 percent when writing calls against stock.

Exhibit 7-2. Convertible bonds hedged by the sale of call options

	Price	*Prices in Six Months*			
Stock	$ 30.00	$ 15	$ 30	$ 45	$ 60
Convertible	122.00	85	122	180	240
Call	3.00	0	0	15	30

Strategy 26: Buy 10 bonds on margin and sell 4 at-the-money calls*

Profit or (loss) on bonds	(3700)	0	5800	11800
Profit or (loss) on calls	1200	1200	(4800)	(10800)
Bond interest received	500	500	500	500
T-bill interest on $1200	60	60	60	60
Total profit or (loss)	(1940)	1760	1560	1560
Return on investment	−15.9%	+14.4%	+12.8%	+12.8%
Annualized return	−31.8%	+28.8%	+25.6%	+25.6%

*Investment = $1220 per bond × 10 bonds = $12200

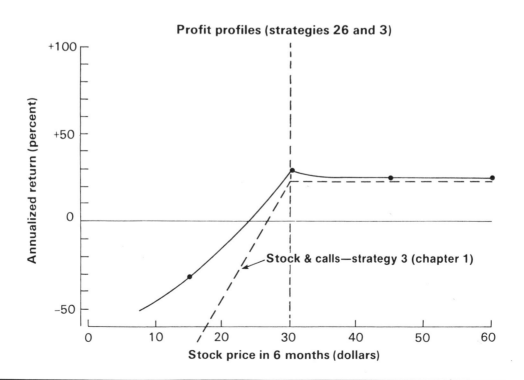

Profit profiles (strategies 26 and 3)

Stock & calls—strategy 3 (chapter 1)

Annualized return (percent)

Stock price in 6 months (dollars)

Assuming that both options are efficiently priced, this call-writing strategy's expected rate of return over the long run should be the same as when protecting convertibles with put options. Option premiums should be evaluated before deciding whether to sell calls or to buy puts. As I illustrated earlier, you should buy puts when premiums are low and sell calls when premiums are high. Don't lock yourself into a single strategy. This advice assumes you don't have a set opinion about the market's near-term direction. If you are a market timer, you can adjust your portfolio as you see fit, without disrupting your core holdings of undervalued securities. Puts and calls may also be used in various combinations for additional portfolio-management flexibility.

HEDGING UNDERVALUED CONVERTIBLES WITH BOTH PUTS AND CALLS

Protecting convertibles with put options is a low-risk strategy, but little or no profits can be expected in the midst of dull, sideways market movements. Selling calls produces profits most of the time, but introduces more risk. Risk-averse investors who would be disappointed if they did not earn some returns during stable markets can employ a long-put/short-call hedge strategy. The strategies illustrated by Exhibits 7-3, 7-4, and 7-5 show bullish, neutral, and bearish hedge postures. These strategies are analogous to the convertible/stock hedges of Chapter 6.

Look first at the bullish hedge of Exhibit 7-3. A purchase of two puts combined with the sale of two calls is similar to shorting 200 shares of stock against the ten bond position (Exhibit 6-2). There are two differences: the premium differential between the put and call, which is credited to the account, provides additional profits; and no short sale dividends are paid. As a result, the put-call combination adds about 5 percent to the convertible/stock hedge yearly returns of Exhibit 6-2. Also included in Exhibit 7-3 is the profit profile for the traditional balanced approach using half common stock and half cash. The lower-risk convertible hedge is expected to outperform the balanced approach at all possible outcomes. It's a heads-you-win, tails-you-don't-lose investment opportunity.

The neutral and bearish strategies of Exhibits 7-4 and 7-5 are even more conservative. They should produce profits regardless of the price the stock closes at on the options' expiration date.

When comparing the option strategies with shorting stock, one might conclude that stocks should never be shorted for protecting convertibles. However, not all attractive convertibles have stocks with listed options, especially the

Exhibit 7-3. Convertible bonds hedged by the purchase of puts and the sale of calls—bullish posture

	Price	*Prices in Six Months*			
Stock	$ 30.00	$ 15	$ 30	$ 45	$ 60
Convertible	122.00	85	122	180	240
Call	3.00	0	0	15	30
Put	1.875	15	0	0	0

Strategy 27: Buy 10 bonds, buy 2 puts, and sell two calls*

Profit or (loss) on bonds	(3700)	0	5800	11800
Profit or (loss) on puts	2625	(375)	(375)	(375)
Profit or (loss) on calls	600	600	(2400)	(5400)
Bond interest received	500	500	500	500
T-bill interest on $225	11	11	11	11
Total profit or (loss)	36	736	3536	6536
Return on investment	+ 0.3%	+ 6.0%	+ 29.0%	+ 53.6%
Annualized return	+ 0.6%	+ 12.0%	+ 58.0%	+ 107.2%

*Investment = $1220 per bond × 10 bonds = $12200

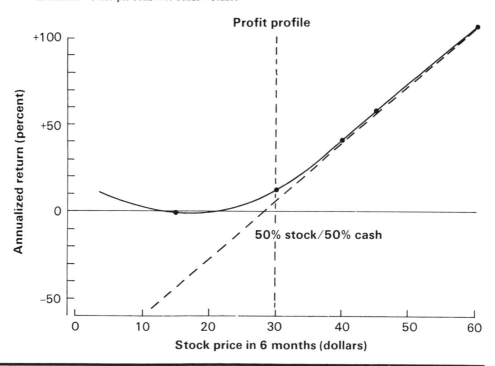

Profit profile

Exhibit 7-4. Convertible bonds hedged by the purchase of puts and the sale of calls—neutral posture

	Price	*Prices in Six Months*			
		$ 15	$ 30	$ 45	$ 60
Stock	$ 30.00	$ 15	$ 30	$ 45	$ 60
Convertible	122.00	85	122	180	240
Call	3.00	0	0	15	30
Put	1.875	15	0	0	0

Strategy 28: Buy 10 bonds, buy 3 puts, and sell 3 calls*

Profit or (loss) on bonds	(3700)	0	5800	11800
Profit or (loss) on puts	3938	(562)	(562)	(562)
Profit or (loss) on calls	900	900	(3600)	(8100)
Bond interest received	500	500	500	500
T-bill interest on $338	17	17	17	17
Total profit or (loss)	1655	855	2155	3655
Return on investment	+13.6%	+ 7.0%	+17.7%	+30.0%
Annualized return	+27.2%	+14.0%	+35.4%	+60.0%

*Investment = $1220 per bond × 10 bonds = $12200

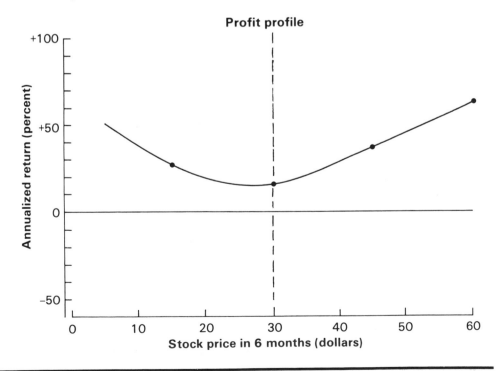

Profit profile

Exhibit 7-5. Convertible bonds hedged by the purchase of puts and the sale of calls—bearish posture

	Price	Prices in Six Months			
Stock	$ 30.00	$ 15	$ 30	$ 45	$ 60
Convertible	122.00	85	122	180	240
Call	3.00	0	0	15	30
Put	1.875	15	0	0	0

Strategy 29: Buy 10 bonds, buy 4 puts, and sell 4 calls*

Profit or (loss) on bonds	(3700)	0	5800	11800
Profit or (loss) on puts	5250	(750)	(750)	(750)
Profit or (loss) on calls	1200	1200	(4800)	(10800)
Bond interest received	500	500	500	500
T-bill interest on $450	22	22	22	22
Total profit or (loss)	3272	972	722	722
Return on investment	+ 26.8%	+ 8.0%	+ 6.3%	+ 6.3%
Annualized return	+ 53.6%	+ 16.0%	+ 12.6%	+ 12.6%

*Investment = $1220 per bond × 10 bonds = $12200

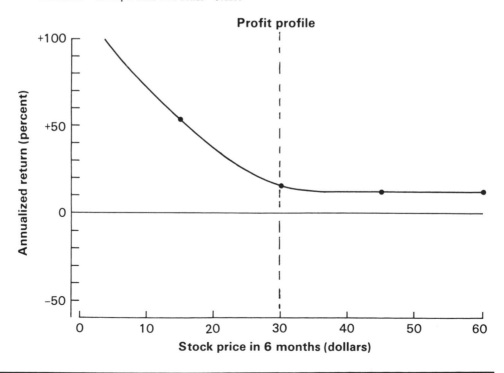

high-performance aggressive convertible bonds of Chapter 5. In addition, the number of option hedgers who use convertibles tends to reduce the amount of undervaluation. Thus, the most attractive issues are usually found in companies which do not have listed options.

Section III's SuperHedging strategies will show how you can gain the advantages of using puts and calls in combination with the most undervalued convertibles available, while incurring lower trading expenses.

SUPERHEDGING

CHAPTER 8

The Components of a SuperHedge Portfolio

Hedging undervalued convertibles allows conservative investors to place most or all of their investment capital in high-performance, equity-related securities. Chapters 6 and 7 demonstrate how to take advantage of attractive market opportunities via low-risk hedging tactics. Profitable as traditional convertible hedging can be for all conservative investors, however, there exists an even better strategy for investors with large portfolios—*SuperHedging*.

I coined the term *SuperHedge* in 1975 while working with a client on an unusual investment concept. Initially, the SuperHedge involved the purchase of dual-purpose fund capital shares, trading at large discounts from their net asset values, in combination with the sale of listed call options on a diversified selection of common stocks.* As a result, we protected the favorably leveraged fund shares with carefully selected (overpriced) calls on unrelated securities. In 1978, I expanded the concept to include portfolios of undervalued convertible securities hedged by the sale of unrelated call options, and/or the purchase of unrelated puts.†

---

* *How the Experts Beat the Market*, Dow Jones-Irwin, 1976.

† *Advanced Investment Strategies*, Dow Jones-Irwin, 1978.

SuperHedging, by allowing one to buy and sell only underpriced or overpriced securities, may be the ultimate hedging strategy. Not only can it reduce risk, it can simultaneously increase returns—the best of both worlds.

THE LONG AND SHORT OF SUPERHEDGING

The core holdings for SuperHedge strategies are diversified portfolios of undervalued, equity-related securities. The best opportunities in the mid-1970s, when the concept was being developed, were the discounted, dual-purpose funds, representing professionally-managed common stock portfolios. Convertible bond portfolios, as illustrated by my firm's low-risk and aggressive indexes (Chapter 5), have offered the best risk-reward relationships in recent years.

Prior to the introduction of index options, core holdings were protected by the purchase of puts and/or the sale of calls on individual common stocks. A $250,000 portfolio of twenty-five different convertible bonds, as an example, might be hedged by twenty-five unrelated call options, each representing $10,000 worth of common stock. Hence, SuperHedgers were required to select and monitor about fifty different security positions. The time and expense were well worth it when overpriced calls could be found. However, as the listed options market became more efficient, the extra time and high brokerage commissions (for executing a large number of small option orders, not for purchasing convertibles) became a deterrent to successful hedging. Unhedged convertibles offered more attractive risk-reward tradeoffs.

Today, SuperHedging is again a viable strategy, and I expect it to offer superior returns for the foreseeable future. The use of index options reduces portfolio-management time and trading expenses. A $250,000 convertible bond portfolio, as an example, can now be protected by a single order of twelve to fifteen index puts or calls. As an extra bonus, there will probably be greater pricing inefficiencies than those previously available for individual stock options, allowing one to buy attractively priced index puts and/or to sell overpriced calls. Let's examine the logic behind this statement.

FINDING INEFFICIENTLY PRICED INDEX OPTIONS

Assuming at-the-money index puts and calls, the normal price difference between the two options reflects the value of risk-free money (Strategy 13 of

Chapter 3). For example, assume that a high-quality index, such as the S&P 500, yields 5 percent when Treasury bills are paying 10 percent.

The fair-value price-spread calculation:
Treasury bill yield for 3 months = 10.0% × 3/12   =   2.50%
Minus S&P 500 yield for 3 months =   5.0% × 3/12   = − 1.25
Price spread = call premium minus put premium   =   1.25%

Since professional investors are likely to have difficulty executing the conversion process with index options, we can expect to see spreads often exceed their theoretical values. Whenever spreads become excessive, we know that either the put is undervalued and/or the call is overpriced. The five probable market conditions associated with a higher-than-normal price spread are:

- highly undervalued puts and modestly undervalued calls
- undervalued puts and normally valued calls
- modestly undervalued puts and modestly overpriced calls
- normally valued puts and overpriced calls
- modestly overpriced puts and highly overpriced calls

The key to successful hedging with index options lies in knowing which condition prevails, since all five pricing combinations present SuperHedging opportunities. When seeking fair-market values, focus attention on the calls to arrive at the correct decision. They continue to be more popular than puts and thus receive closer scrutiny by the option-evaluation services. Let's look again at three-month calls on the S&P 500 as a starting point.

PROTECTING THE S&P 500 WITH INDEX OPTIONS

In recent years, Treasury bill rates of return have fluctuated around the 10 percent level, and the S&P 500 has yielded about 5 percent—the figures I used in the example for calculating the normal put-call price spread. By studying actual market prices, and through probability analysis, I tentatively concluded that a three month call on the S&P index should probably trade in the 3.5 to 4 percent range. To test this assumption under actual market conditions, I prepared Table 8-1, based on call premiums of 3.75 percent and puts at 2.5 percent. The study was extended back to 1976 to permit a direct comparison with our convertible bond indexes. Thirty-six quarterly performance numbers should provide a meaningful test of my premium-level assumptions.

Table 8-1. Quarterly returns for the S&P 500 index if hedged by three-month at-the-money, normally valued index puts and calls—1976–84.

Year	Qtr	T-bills	S&P 500	S&P 500 *	long puts	short calls
1976	1	+ 1.2%	+ 14.0%	+ 15.0%	+ 12.5%	+ 4.8%
	2	+ 1.3	+ 1.4	+ 2.4	− 0.1	+ 4.8
	3	+ 1.3	+ 0.9	+ 1.9	− 0.6	+ 4.8
	4	+ 1.2	+ 2.1	+ 3.1	+ 0.6	+ 4.8
1977	1	+ 1.1	− 8.7	− 7.5	− 1.3	− 3.8
	2	+ 1.2	+ 2.0	+ 3.2	+ 0.7	+ 5.0
	3	+ 1.3	− 4.0	− 2.8	− 1.3	+ 1.0
	4	+ 1.5	− 1.5	− 0.3	− 1.3	+ 3.4
1978	1	+ 1.6	− 6.3	− 4.9	− 1.1	− 1.2
	2	+ 1.6	+ 7.1	+ 8.5	+ 6.0	+ 5.2
	3	+ 1.8	+ 7.3	+ 8.7	+ 6.2	+ 5.2
	4	+ 2.0	− 6.4	− 5.0	− 1.1	− 1.2
1979	1	+ 2.3	+ 5.7	+ 7.1	+ 4.6	+ 5.2
	2	+ 2.3	+ 1.3	+ 2.7	+ 0.2	+ 5.2
	3	+ 2.3	+ 6.2	+ 7.6	+ 5.1	+ 5.2
	4	+ 2.8	− 1.3	+ 0.1	− 1.1	+ 3.8
1980	1	+ 3.1	− 5.4	− 4.1	− 1.2	− 0.4
	2	+ 2.7	+ 12.2	+ 13.5	+ 11.0	+ 5.0
	3	+ 2.1	+ 9.9	+ 11.2	+ 8.7	+ 5.0
	4	+ 3.1	+ 8.2	+ 9.5	+ 7.0	+ 5.0
1981	1	+ 3.4	+ 0.1	+ 1.4	− 1.1	+ 5.0
	2	+ 3.5	− 3.6	− 2.3	− 1.2	+ 1.4
	3	+ 3.7	− 11.6	− 10.3	− 1.2	− 6.6
	4	+ 3.0	+ 5.6	+ 6.9	+ 4.4	+ 5.0
1982	1	+ 3.1	− 8.6	− 7.3	− 1.2	− 3.6
	2	+ 3.0	− 1.9	− 0.6	− 1.2	+ 3.2
	3	+ 2.4	+ 10.2	+ 11.5	+ 9.0	+ 5.0
	4	+ 2.0	+ 16.9	+ 18.2	+ 15.7	+ 5.0
1983	1	+ 2.0	+ 8.8	+ 10.0	+ 7.5	+ 5.0
	2	+ 2.1	+ 9.9	+ 11.1	+ 8.6	+ 5.0
	3	+ 2.3	− 1.4	− 0.2	− 1.3	+ 3.6
	4	+ 2.2	− 0.8	+ 0.4	− 1.3	+ 4.2
1984	1	+ 2.3	− 3.6	− 2.4	− 1.3	+ 1.4
	2	+ 2.4	− 3.8	− 2.6	− 1.3	+ 1.2
	3	+ 2.6	+ 8.5	+ 9.7	+ 7.2	+ 5.0
	4	+ 2.3	+ 0.6	+ 1.8	− 0.7	+ 5.0

*Includes dividends ranging from 4.0 to 5.6 percent annually.
 calls = 3.75%, puts = 2.5%

Calculations of hypothetical option-hedging performance figures in Table 8-1 (1976 first quarter data, columns 6 and 7):

Put hedge quarterly return = S&P 500 return – put premium paid +
put's intrinsic value at expiration
= +15.0% –2.5% +0%
= +12.5%

Call hedge quarterly return = S&P 500 return × call premium rec'd –
call's intrinsic value at expiration
= +15.0% +3.75% – 14.0%
= +4.75% (4.8% rounded)

Notice that the options' intrinsic values at expiration are based on price action of the S & P 500 excluding dividends (column 4). With an index gain of 14 percent, the put would end up at 0 and the call at 14 percent of the index. Investors holding the index's underlying stocks would earn 15 percent when adding in the prevailing 1 percent quarterly yield.

The study assumes constant option premiums over the nine-year period to simplify the calculations. However, as I indicated earlier, premiums should vary along with T-bill rates of return. When T-bill rates were lower than my assumptions, as they were during the early years of the study, the hedging performance calculations are overstated; when rates were higher, they are understated. The study excludes interest earned on call premiums received and interest charges on puts purchased, again to simplify the calculations.

Averaging the returns of the two hedging strategies results in a revealing calculation. Let's look at a hypothetical quarter, assuming T-bill and stock market yields are precisely at our 10 and 5 percent assumptions and based on a total return of 6 percent for the S&P. The columns of Table 8-1 would look like this:

T-bills	S&P 500	S&P 500*	long puts	short calls
+ 2.5%	+ 4.75%	+ 6.0%	+ 3.5%	+ 5.0%

The sum of the two hedging returns (3.5 + 5.0 = 8.5) equals the sum of T-bills and the S&P 500 with dividends (2.5 + 6.0 = 8.5). In effect, the put-call combination is the same as employing the conversion process for half of one's portfolio and unhedged S&P stocks for the other half—the middle of the option-strategies line (Exhibit 2-7). To achieve on- or above-the-line performance after trading expenses, hedgers must purchase only undervalued puts and/or sell overpriced calls; a lower-cost alternative is to simply buy and hold a portfolio of common stocks in combination with a money market fund.

There have been indications that the option income funds may switch to selling index calls instead of selling calls on individual stocks. While this tactic should lower their portfolio-turnover costs, I have no doubt they will continue to underperform the passive T-bill/common-stock balanced approach. Their only chance for success is to find overpriced calls, but premiums already appear to be about normally valued without their participation.

RISK-REWARD ANALYSIS

Table 8-2 presents annual performance data for the index-option strategies, including standard-deviation and coefficient-of-variation calculations similar to analyses of the convertible bond indexes (Chapter 5). Annualized returns versus coefficients of variation are graphed by Exhibits 8-1 and 8-2; Treasury bills and Standard & Poor's 500 stock index are included for comparison.

First, review the five-year data of Table 8-2 and Exhibit 8-1. While hedging with puts did somewhat better than selling calls, neither strategy produced above-the-line performance. The annualized average of the two hedging tactics (12.75 percent) was slightly below the T-bill/common-stock combination (12.95 percent), and hedging experienced a modestly higher risk level. The small performance difference can probably be attributed to my 10 percent T-bill yield assumption compared to an 11.1 percent average for the five-year period.

The nine-year data of Table 8-2 and Exhibit 8-2 favored the call-writing strategy: call-option hedging provided above-the-line performance. In addition, the put-call average (11.55 percent) exceeded T-bills and stocks (10.85 percent). Part of the extra return from hedging can be explained by the lower 9.2 percent T-bill average rate compared to my 10 percent assumption for the nine years— the put-call combination also experienced higher risk than did T-bills/common stocks.

Table 8-2. Annual returns for the S & P 500 index if hedged by three-month at-the-money, normally valued index puts and calls—1976–84

Year	T-bills	S&P 500	long puts	short calls
1976	+ 5.1%	+ 23.6%	+ 12.4%	+ 20.4%
1977	+ 5.2	− 7.2	− 3.2	+ 5.5
1978	+ 7.1	+ 6.6	+ 10.1	+ 7.9
1979	+ 10.0	+ 18.4	+ 8.9	+ 20.7
1980	+ 11.4	+ 32.5	+ 27.6	+ 15.5
1981	+ 14.2	− 5.0	+ 0.8	+ 4.6
1982	+ 10.9	+ 21.6	+ 23.1	+ 9.8
1983	+ 8.9	+ 22.5	+ 13.7	+ 18.8
1984	+ 9.9	+ 6.2	+ 3.7	+ 12.9
Last 5-year data				
Cumulative return	69%	99%	87%	78%
Annualized return	11.1	14.8	13.3	12.2
Average quarterly return	2.7	3.8	3.3	3.0
Standard deviation	0.5	7.8	5.5	3.3
Coefficient of variation	20	205	165	110
9-year data				
Cumulative return	120%	188%	144%	194%
Annualized return	9.2	12.5	10.4	12.7
Average quarterly return	2.2	3.2	2.6	3.1
Standard deviation	0.7	7.0	4.9	3.1
Coeffficient of variation	32	216	186	99

Calls = 3.75%, puts = 2.5%

Although call writing outperformed the purchased-put alternative over the longer nine-year period, I am not prepared to conclude that the 3.75 and 2.5 percent premium assumptions were too high. The time frame covered by the analysis was a nearly perfect market environment for any covered-call-writing strategy. More volatile markets, such as the 1973–74 selloff and the subsequent strong recovery in 1975, would have favored purchasing puts (look at the worst and the best stock-market quarters of Tables 8-1). Selling calls is best during stable or modestly rising markets—puts will work best in up or down volatile markets.

Exhibit 8-1. Risk-reward analysis for Standard & Poor's 500 hedged by index options, 5 years (1980–84)

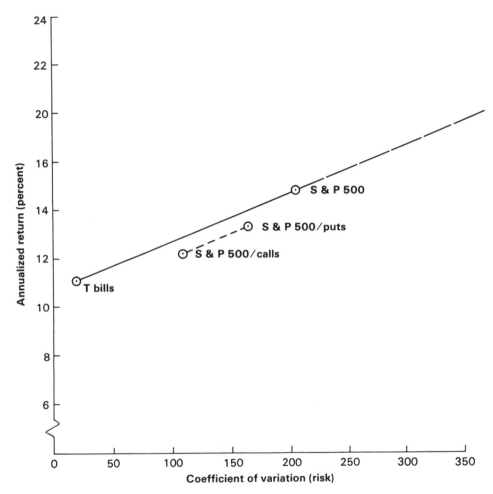

PROTECTING SPECULATIVE STOCKS WITH INDEX OPTIONS

The S&P 500 is one of the highest-quality indexes available; the American Stock Exchange index (AMEX) is probably the most speculative. Most stock portfolios will likely fall somewhere between these extremes. Therefore, investors

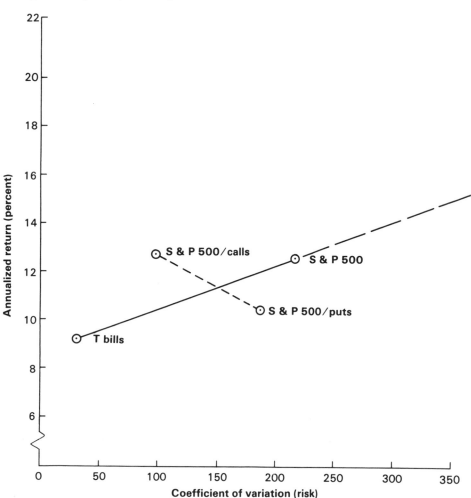

Exhibit 8-2. Risk-reward analysis for Standard & Poor's 500 hedged by index options, 9 years (1976–84)

attempting to match their specific portfolios with appropriate index options should consider mixing options on the S&P 500 with those on the AMEX or other broad-based indexes. The possible combinations are virtually unlimited, depending on trading liquidity.

Tables 8-3 and 8-4 and Exhibits 8-3 and 8-4 present data for hedging the AMEX index based on premium assumptions of 6 and 3.5 percent for calls and

Table 8-3. Quarterly returns for the AMEX index if hedged by three-month at-the-money, normally-valued index puts and calls—1976–84.

Year	Qtr	AMEX*	long puts	short calls
1976	1	+ 24.9%	+ 21.4%	+ 6.0%
	2	+ 1.0	− 2.5	+ 6.0
	3	− 3.2	− 3.5	+ 2.8
	4	+ 7.7	+ 4.2	+ 6.0
1977	1	+ 1.2	− 2.3	+ 6.0
	2	+ 8.2	+ 4.7	+ 6.0
	3	− 1.2	− 3.5	+ 4.8
	4	+ 7.6	+ 4.1	+ 6.0
1978	1	+ 0.8	− 2.7	+ 6.0
	2	+ 12.9	+ 9.4	+ 6.0
	3	+ 16.0	+ 12.5	+ 6.0
	4	− 10.8	− 3.5	− 4.8
1979	1	+ 19.4	+ 15.9	+ 6.0
	2	+ 11.7	+ 8.2	+ 6.0
	3	+ 2.2	− 1.3	+ 6.0
	4	+ 20.4	+ 16.9	+ 6.0
1980	1	− 5.7	− 3.5	+ 0.3
	2	+ 26.0	+ 22.5	+ 6.0
	3	+ 12.9	+ 9.4	+ 6.0
	4	+ 5.3	+ 1.8	+ 6.0
1981	1	+ 3.3	− 0.2	+ 6.0
	2	+ 3.9	+ 0.4	+ 6.0
	3	− 21.8	− 3.5	− 15.8
	4	+ 9.5	+ 6.0	+ 6.0
1982	1	− 18.9	− 3.5	− 12.9
	2	− 3.6	− 3.5	+ 2.4
	3	+ 12.9	+ 9.4	+ 6.0
	4	+ 20.3	+ 16.8	+ 6.0
1983	1	+ 14.2	+ 10.7	+ 6.0
	2	+ 24.6	+ 21.1	+ 6.0
	3	− 5.0	− 3.5	+ 1.0
	4	− 3.1	− 3.5	+ 2.9
1984	1	− 5.4	− 3.5	+ 0.6
	2	− 5.1	− 3.5	+ 0.9
	3	+ 7.6	+ 4.1	+ 6.0
	4	− 5.2	− 3.5	+ 0.8

*The AMEX index includes dividends
Calls = 6.0%, puts = 3.5%

Table 8-4. Annual returns for the AMEX index if hedged by three-month at-the-money, normally valued index puts and calls—1976–84

Year	T-bills	AMEX	long puts	short calls
1976	+ 5.1%	+ 31.6%	+ 19.0%	+ 22.4%
1977	+ 5.2	+ 16.4	+ 2.8	+ 24.8
1978	+ 7.1	+ 17.7	+ 15.6	+ 13.4
1979	+ 10.0	+ 64.4	+ 44.7	+ 26.2
1980	+ 11.4	+ 41.2	+ 31.7	+ 19.5
1981	+ 14.2	− 8.1	+ 2.5	+ 2.8
1982	+ 10.9	+ 6.2	+ 19.0	+ 2.1
1983	+ 8.9	+ 31.0	+ 24.8	+ 16.8
1984	+ 9.9	− 8.4	− 6.5	+ 8.5
Last 5-year data				
Cumulative return	69%	65%	88%	54%
Annualized return	11.1	10.5	13.5	9.0
Average quarterly return	2.7	3.3	3.5	2.3
Standard deviation	0.5	13.0	8.7	6.2
Coefficient of variation	20	389	247	
9-year data				
Cumulative return	120%	389%	284%	233%
Annualized return	9.2	19.3	16.1	14.3
Average quarterly return	2.2	5.1	4.1	3.5
Standard deviation	0.7	11.7	8.4	5.1
Coefficient of variation	32	226	205	144

Calls = 6.0%, puts = 3.5%

puts respectively. These higher premiums were chosen to reflect the AMEX's more volatile nature. Since the AMEX includes dividends paid by its underlying stocks, the 2.5 percent price spread equals risk-free Treasury bill rates of return for three months.

As shown by the data, the AMEX index-option hedges produced results similar to hedges on the S&P 500 except they did relatively better over the last five-year period, when speculative stocks performed poorly (Exhibit 8-3). However, the put and call hedges could not keep pace with high-flying AMEX stocks during the early years of the study—nine-year returns both fell below-the-line (Exhibit 8-4).

Exhibit 8-3. Risk-reward analysis for the AMEX index hedged by index options, 5 years (1980–84)

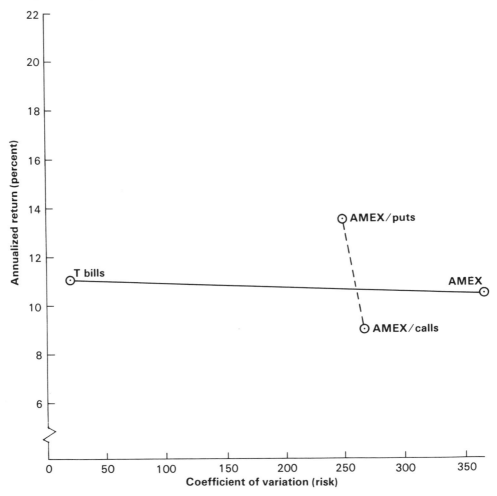

These hypothetical index-option studies help to confirm that normally valued puts and calls in combination with common stocks will not enhance investment performance. After deducting management fees and trading expenses, below-the-line results can be anticipated.

Let's now move on to SuperHedging strategies involving both undervalued and overvalued securities. Chapter 9 will evaluate low-risk convertible bonds protected by inefficiently priced index options.

Exhibit 8-4. Risk-reward analysis for the AMEX index hedged by index options, 9 years (1976–84)

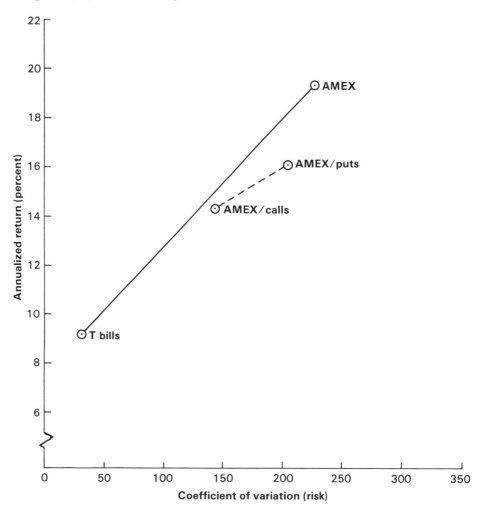

SuperHedge Strategies with Low-Risk Convertibles

In the Introduction I said that equity hedging must compensate for the extra time and expense through higher returns. Chapters 2 and 8 demonstrate why common stock portfolios hedged with normally valued puts and calls cannot be expected to improve investment results. These chapters point out that extra time and expense are, in fact, usually rewarded by lower returns. Brokers and marketmakers are the only winners.

In Chapter 2 I pointed out that winning option strategies are available to astute, noninstitutional-sized investors. This chapter introduces the unorthodox investment concept of SuperHedging with index options and convertible securities. I will show how you can use carefully chosen index puts and calls in combination with attractive convertibles to simultaneously increase returns and reduce risk. You will be amply compensated for the extra time and expense incurred from implementing these advanced strategies.

Core holdings for this chapter's SuperHedge strategies are undervalued, high-quality convertibles. I use the Noddings-Calamos low-risk convertible bond index (Chapter 5) as the proxy for testing historical performance data, and the popular puts and calls on the S&P 100 for the other side of the hedges.

The S&P 100 closely tracks the performance of the S&P 500, as do other high-quality indexes: the AMEX Major Market Index and the NYSE Composite Index (Chapter 3). All four of these broad-based market indicators may be employed for hedging low-risk convertibles; future performance differences among them will probably not be substantial. In any event, their future variances are unpredictable.

Before presenting low-risk SuperHedging using undervalued puts and over-priced calls, let's look at the strategies based on normally valued options.

HEDGING LOW-RISK CONVERTIBLES WITH EFFICIENTLY PRICED S&P 100 INDEX OPTIONS

Tables 9-1 and 9-2 provide hypothetical performance results using undervalued, low-risk convertibles and normally valued, three-month S&P 100 puts and calls trading at premiums of 2.5 and 3.75 percent, respectively—the same as the S&P 500 option-premium assumptions of Chapter 8. Three hedging strategies using at-the-money options are evaluated: convertibles protected by long puts, convertibles protected by short calls, and convertibles protected by puts and calls in combination. In effect, the put-call combination fabricates a short sale on the market covering half of the portfolio—its risk-reward characteristics are similar to the bullish, half-hedge posture of Strategy 19 (Exhibit 6-2).

As would be expected when employing fairly priced options, the hedge results show lower risk, but also lower rates of return, than unhedged convertibles—the same risk-reward relationships as the traditional convert-ible/option hedging strategies of Chapter 7. The single exception, as in Chapter 8, was the higher performance when selling calls over the full nine-year period.

Looking at the quarterly calculations of Table 9-1, we can see divergences between the low-risk convertibles and the S&P 100. Most variations were positive (the convertibles did better than the S&P); and, as expected, a few quarters were negative. During 1980's fourth quarter, as a worst case example, the S&P 100 advanced 7.3 percent while low-risk convertibles barely gained 0.2 percent. All three hedging strategies lost money during a good stock-market quarter. However, when the following two quarters saw the convertibles

Table 9-1. Quarterly returns for the Noddings-Calamos low-risk convertible bond index if hedged by three-month at-the-money, normally-valued index puts and calls—1976–84

Year	Quarter	S&P 100	Low-risk convertible bond index	Strategy 30 long puts	Strategy 30 short calls	Strategy 32 puts & calls
1976	1	+ 13.1%	+ 18.0%	+ 15.5%	+ 8.6%	+ 12.0%
	2	+ 0.8	+ 4.9	+ 2.4	+ 7.8	+ 5.1
	3	+ 1.4	+ 5.5	+ 3.0	+ 7.8	+ 5.4
	4	+ 0.7	+ 6.1	+ 3.6	+ 9.2	+ 6.4
1977	1	− 9.2	− 1.4	+ 5.3	+ 2.4	+ 3.8
	2	+ 1.7	+ 6.2	+ 3.7	+ 8.2	+ 6.0
	3	− 3.1	− 1.3	− 0.7	+ 2.4	+ 0.9
	4	− 2.1	+ 1.4	+ 1.0	+ 5.2	+ 3.1
1978	1	− 7.3	+ 2.4	+ 7.2	+ 6.2	+ 6.7
	2	+ 8.2	+ 11.1	+ 8.6	+ 6.6	+ 7.6
	3	+ 7.9	+ 8.1	+ 5.6	+ 4.0	+ 4.8
	4	− 4.0	− 9.8	− 8.3	− 6.0	− 7.2
1979	1	+ 4.4	+ 9.3	+ 6.8	+ 8.6	+ 7.7
	2	− 1.1	+ 6.8	+ 5.4	+ 10.6	+ 8.0
	3	+ 4.1	+ 6.0	+ 3.5	+ 5.6	+ 4.6
	4	− 2.6	− 3.1	− 3.0	+ 0.6	− 1.2
1980	1	− 4.1	− 6.5	− 4.9	− 2.8	− 3.8
	2	+ 9.4	+ 20.7	+ 18.2	+ 15.0	+ 16.6
	3	+ 10.0	+ 14.2	+ 11.7	+ 8.0	+ 9.8
	4	+ 7.3	+ 0.2	− 2.3	− 3.4	− 2.8
1981	1	− 0.7	+ 7.6	+ 5.8	+ 11.4	+ 8.6
	2	− 4.2	+ 4.8	+ 6.5	+ 8.6	+ 7.5
	3	− 11.5	− 9.9	− 0.9	− 6.2	− 3.5
	4	+ 3.2	+ 10.9	+ 8.4	+ 11.4	+ 9.9
1982	1	− 7.0	− 5.7	− 1.2	− 2.0	− 1.6
	2	− 1.5	− 3.4	− 4.4	+ 0.4	− 2.0
	3	+ 9.8	+ 11.6	+ 9.1	+ 5.6	+ 7.3
	4	+ 18.2	+ 12.9	+ 10.4	− 1.6	+ 4.4
1983	1	+ 8.2	+ 13.0	+ 10.5	+ 8.6	+ 9.5
	2	+ 9.6	+ 12.2	+ 9.7	+ 6.4	+ 8.0
	3	− 0.9	− 1.6	− 3.2	+ 2.2	− 0.5
	4	− 0.6	− 2.2	− 4.1	+ 1.6	− 1.3
1984	1	− 5.6	− 1.4	+ 1.7	+ 2.4	+ 2.0
	2	− 3.1	− 1.5	− 0.9	+ 2.2	+ 0.7
	3	+ 8.8	+ 6.6	+ 4.1	+ 1.6	+ 2.8
	4	− 0.1	+ 2.2	− 0.2	+ 6.0	+ 2.9

Calls = 3.75%, puts = 2.5%

Table 9-2. The Noddings-Calamos low-risk convertible bond index and hedging strategies using normally-valued S&P 100 index options—1976–84

Year	S&P 500	Low-risk convertible bond index	Strategy 30 long puts	Strategy 31 short calls	Strategy 32 puts & calls
1976	+ 23.6%	+ 38.6%	+ 26.1%	+ 37.8%	+ 32.0%
1977	− 7.2	+ 4.8	+ 9.5	+ 19.4	+ 14.5
1978	+ 6.6	+ 10.9	+ 12.7	+ 10.7	+ 11.7
1979	+ 18.4	+ 19.9	+ 13.0	+ 27.6	+ 20.2
1980	+ 32.5	+ 29.1	+ 22.7	+ 16.6	+ 19.7
1981	− 5.0	+ 12.7	+ 21.0	+ 26.4	+ 23.8
1982	+ 21.6	+ 14.8	+ 13.8	+ 2.2	+ 8.0
1983	+ 22.5	+ 22.0	+ 12.5	+ 20.0	+ 16.1
1984	+ 6.2	+ 5.8	+ 4.7	+ 12.7	+ 8.7

Last 5-year data

Cumulative return		116%	99%	104%	102%
Annualized return		16.7	14.8	15.3	15.1
Average quarterly return		4.2	3.7	3.8	3.7
Standard deviation		8.4	6.6	5.6	5.7
Coefficient of variation		198	179	150	153

9-year data

Cumulative return		316%	250%	373%	310%
Annualized return		17.2	14.9	18.8	17.0
Average quarterly return		4.3	3.7	4.5	4.1
Standard deviation		7.5	6.0	5.0	5.1
Coefficient of variation		174	161	111	124

Calls = 3.75%, puts = 2.5%

advance while the S&P 100 declined, the hedging strategies were extremely profitable. These performance divergences are to be expected from time to time, since the two sides of the hedge portfolio involve different underlying common stocks.

Serious investors take a realistic view towards the markets by recognizing that although abnormal events will occur, they average out over the long run. Short-term performance measurements, good or bad, are at best meaningless; at worst they encourage nervous investors to make poor decisions. Sophisticated hedging strategies should be pursued only by knowledgeable and patient investors. Having said that, let's now visit the esoteric world of SuperHedging. As you enter, close the door behind you; you may never return to the other world of conventional investing.

HEDGING LOW-RISK CONVERTIBLES WITH INEFFICIENTLY PRICED S&P 100 INDEX OPTIONS

The calculations of Tables 9-3 and 9-4 are similar to those just studied (Tables 9-1 and 9-2), except I have increased the call option premium from 3.75 percent to 4.25 percent and dropped the put premium from 2.5 percent to 2 percent. Representing what I believe would be modestly overpriced calls and modestly underpriced puts, the extra .5 percent profit either adds to each quarter's hedge returns or it reduces losses. Since both options are assumed to be inefficiently priced, each of the three different hedge strategies should produce high risk-adjusted returns over the long term.

From Table 9-4, notice that all three hedging strategies outperformed the unhedged convertibles during both the five- and nine-year periods. As was expected, hedging with inefficiently priced options enhanced returns: risk, as measured by the coefficient of variation, was reduced substantially.

Comparing the standard deviation numbers of Table 9-4 with those of Table 9-2 results in an interesting observation. They are identical—further evidence that the standard deviation is not the best measurement of risk! By selecting inefficiently priced options, we are able to add to each quarter's return; but variability, as calculated by the standard deviation, remained the same. The coefficients of variation adjust for these ambiguities and correctly show lower risk factors for each of the hedging strategies of Table 9-4.

Exhibits 9-1 and 9-2 graphically illustrate how SuperHedging with modestly undervalued puts and modestly overpriced calls can produce above-the-line performance. However, real-world opportunities to find even greater pricing inefficiencies, as I indicated in Chapter 8, do exist.

The nine-year data graphed in Exhibit 9-2 reveal that the annualized returns for the lower-risk hedging strategies ranged from about 2 percentage points above the line connecting T-bills and unhedged convertibles to about 8 percentage points. Even with brokerage commission deductions for the options, which

Table 9-3. Quarterly returns for the Noddings-Calamos low-risk convertible bond index if hedged by three-month S&P 100 at-the-money, *undervalued* index puts and/or *overpriced* calls—1976–84

Year	Quarter	S&P 100	Low-risk convertible bond index	Strategy 30 long puts	Strategy 31 short calls	Strategy 32 puts & calls
1976	1	+ 13.1%	+ 18.0%	+ 16.0%	+ 9.2%	+ 12.6%
	2	+ 0.8	+ 4.9	+ 2.9	+ 8.4	+ 5.6
	3	+ 1.4	+ 5.5	+ 3.5	+ 8.4	+ 5.9
	4	+ 0.7	+ 6.1	+ 4.1	+ 9.6	+ 6.9
1977	1	− 9.2	− 1.4	+ 5.8	+ 2.8	+ 4.3
	2	+ 1.7	+ 6.2	+ 4.2	+ 8.8	+ 6.5
	3	− 3.1	− 1.3	− 0.2	+ 3.0	+ 1.4
	4	− 2.1	+ 1.4	+ 1.5	+ 5.6	+ 3.6
1978	1	− 7.3	+ 2.4	+ 7.7	+ 6.6	+ 7.2
	2	+ 8.2	+ 11.1	+ 9.1	+ 7.2	+ 8.1
	3	+ 7.9	+ 8.1	+ 6.1	+ 4.4	+ 5.3
	4	− 4.0	− 9.8	− 7.8	− 5.6	− 6.7
1979	1	+ 4.4	+ 9.3	+ 7.3	+ 9.2	+ 8.2
	2	− 1.1	+ 6.8	+ 5.9	+ 11.0	+ 8.5
	3	+ 4.1	+ 6.0	+ 4.0	+ 6.2	+ 5.1
	4	− 2.6	− 3.1	− 2.5	+ 1.2	− 0.7
1980	1	− 4.1	− 6.5	− 4.4	− 2.2	− 3.3
	2	+ 9.4	+ 20.7	+ 18.7	+ 15.6	+ 17.1
	3	+ 10.0	+ 14.2	+ 12.2	+ 8.4	+ 10.3
	4	+ 7.3	+ 0.2	− 1.8	− 2.8	− 2.3
1981	1	− 0.7	+ 7.6	+ 6.3	+ 11.8	+ 9.1
	2	− 4.2	+ 4.8	+ 7.0	+ 9.0	+ 8.0
	3	− 11.5	− 9.9	− 0.4	− 5.6	− 3.0
	4	+ 3.2	+ 10.9	+ 8.9	+ 12.0	+ 10.4
1982	1	− 7.0	− 5.7	− 0.7	− 1.4	− 1.1
	2	− 1.5	− 3.4	− 3.9	+ 0.8	− 1.5
	3	+ 9.8	+ 11.6	+ 9.6	+ 6.0	+ 7.8
	4	+ 18.2	+ 12.9	+ 10.9	− 1.0	+ 4.9
1983	1	+ 8.2	+ 13.0	+ 11.0	+ 9.0	+ 10.0
	2	+ 9.6	+ 12.2	+ 10.2	+ 6.8	+ 8.5
	3	− 0.9	− 1.6	− 2.7	+ 2.6	0
	4	− 0.6	− 2.2	− 3.6	+ 2.0	− 0.8
1984	1	− 5.6	− 1.4	+ 2.2	+ 2.8	+ 2.5
	2	− 3.1	− 1.5	− 0.4	+ 2.8	+ 1.2
	3	+ 8.8	+ 6.6	+ 4.6	+ 2.0	+ 3.3
	4	− 0.1	+ 2.2	+ 0.3	+ 6.4	+ 3.4

Calls = 4.25%, puts = 2.0%

Table 9-4. The Noddings-Calamos low-risk convertible bond index and hedging strategies using *undervalued* S&P 100 index puts and/or *overpriced* calls—1976–84

Year calls	S&P 500	Low-risk convertible bond index	Strategy 30 long puts	Strategy 31 short calls	Strategy 32 puts & calls
1976	+ 23.6%	+ 38.6%	+ 28.6%	+ 40.6%	+ 34.6%
1977	− 7.2	+ 4.8	+ 11.7	+ 21.7	+ 16.7
1978	+ 6.6	+ 10.9	+ 14.9	+ 12.6	+ 13.8
1979	+ 18.4	+ 19.9	+ 15.2	+ 30.3	+ 22.5
1980	+ 32.5	+ 29.1	+ 25.0	+ 19.1	+ 22.0
1981	− 5.0	+ 12.7	+ 23.4	+ 28.8	+ 26.2
1982	+ 21.6	+ 14.8	+ 16.0	+ 4.3	+ 10.2
1983	+ 22.5	+ 22.0	+ 14.7	+ 21.8	+ 18.4
1984	+ 6.2	+ 5.8	+ 6.8	+ 14.7	+ 10.8
Last 5-year data					
Cumulative return		116%	119%	124%	123%
Annualized return		16.7	17.0	17.5	17.4
Average quarterly return		4.2	4.2	4.2	4.2
Standard deviation		8.4	6.6	5.6	5.7
Coefficient of variation		198	158	132	135
9-year data					
Cumulative return		316%	317%	461%	387%
Annualized return		17.2	17.2	21.1	19.2
Average quarterly return		4.3	4.2	5.0	4.6
Standard deviation		7.5	6.0	5.0	5.1
Coefficient of variation		174	142	100	110

Calls = 4.25%, puts = 2.0%

should usually fall well below .5 percent per year of the total portfolio's value, the risk-reward enhancements are substantial. SuperHedging strategies far outdistanced the conventional returns from common stocks and money-market instruments represented by the lower line of Exhibit 9-2. This is what sophisticated investing is all about.

Exhibit 9-1. Risk-reward analysis for low-risk convertible bond strategies using index options, 5 years (1980–84)

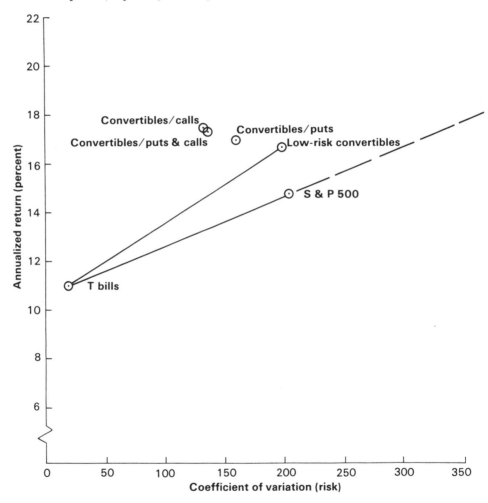

Exhibit 9-2. Risk-reward analysis for low-risk convertible bond strategies using index options, 9 years (1976–84)

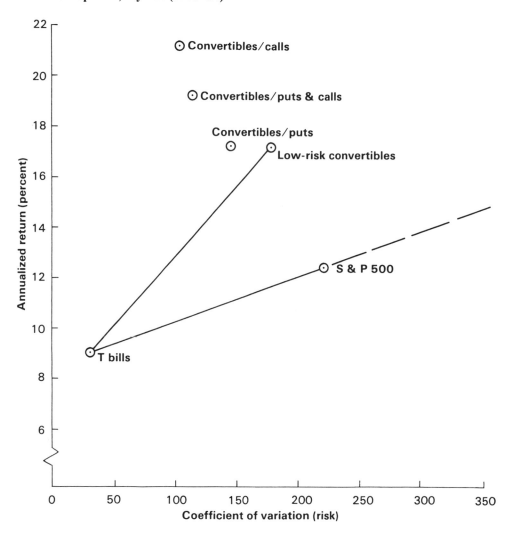

CHAPTER 10

SuperHedge Strategies with Aggressive Convertibles

Over the years, small company stocks have outperformed those of large companies. It is logical to expect that convertible bonds of smaller firms would also have done well. In actual practice, carefully selected convertibles issued by low-cap companies have outperformed their underlying stocks at far lower levels of risk (Chapter 5). I never cease to be amazed, however, at how quickly investors reject B rated convertible bonds, only to turn around and purchase B (or lower) rated stocks. They have been indoctrinated to believe that safety of principal is the primary consideration when buying bonds, but that seeking high capital appreciation is acceptable and desirable when buying common stocks. Most investors never assess the risk-reward characteristics of their total portfolios.

The coefficient-of-variation calculations in Chapter 5 show that high-performing, aggressive convertible bonds have been even less risky than either blue chip common stocks or high-quality bonds. Yet, most investors will not opt for portfolios of such low-quality securities. Recognizing that acceptance of speculative convertible bonds is a difficult decision for conservative investors, this chapter presents strategies that will permit these investors to receive the full benefits aggressive convertibles can offer, while reducing risk to a point well below that of high-quality stocks and bonds. Like the SuperHedge strategies of Chapter 9, these strategies hedge aggressive convertible bonds with index puts and calls.

HEDGING AGGRESSIVE CONVERTIBLES WITH INEFFICIENTLY PRICED S&P 100 INDEX OPTIONS

As I stress throughout this book, the most undervalued securities are usually found in the market niches least attractive to institutional investors. Typically, low-quality convertibles, lacking both high trading liquidity and investment grade characteristics, are ignored by institutional money managers.

Chapter 7 illustrates that carefully selected convertible bonds are ideal candidates for traditional, low-risk hedging strategies using listed puts and calls. However, the majority of attractive convertibles are issued by companies without listed options trading on their stocks. Of the twenty-five issues making up the Noddings-Calamos aggressive convertible bond index at the end of 1984 (Table 5-4), for instance, only one company had listed options. Index options are the answer to this dilemma.

Tables 10-1 and 10-2 present hypothetical performance results for the Noddings-Calamos aggressive convertible bond index when hedged with S&P 100 put and call options, beginning in 1976. I make the same assumptions as in Chapter 9 for hedging my firm's low-risk convertible index: modestly undervalued puts at 2 percent and modestly overpriced calls at 4.25 percent. The same three SuperHedge strategies are also evaluated: convertibles protected by long puts, convertibles protected by short calls, and convertibles protected by puts and calls in combination.

All three SuperHedges would have produced high rates of return at risk levels lower than unhedged convertibles. Call writing was again the best performing of the three strategies over the full nine-year period; by including no bear markets, this time frame represents a nearly perfect market environment for selling call options.

Comparing the aggressive convertible SuperHedges (Table 10-2) with those of low-risk convertibles (Table 9-4), it is interesting to observe that their

Table 10–1. Quarterly returns for the Noddings-Calamos aggressive convertible bond index if hedged by three-month S&P 100 at-the-money, *undervalued* index puts and/or *overpriced* calls—1976–84.

Year	Quarter	S&P 100	Aggressive convertible bond index	Strategy 33 long puts	Strategy 34 short calls	Strategy 35 puts & calls
1976	1	+ 13.1%	+ 9.7%	+ 7.7%	+ 0.8%	+ 4.3%
	2	+ 0.8	+ 9.0	+ 7.0	+ 12.4	+ 9.7
	3	+ 1.4	+ 6.1	+ 4.1	+ 9.0	+ 6.5
	4	+ 0.7	+ 4.9	+ 2.9	+ 8.4	+ 5.7
1977	1	− 9.2	+ 1.5	+ 8.7	+ 5.8	+ 7.2
	2	+ 1.7	+ 4.9	+ 2.9	+ 7.4	+ 5.2
	3	− 3.1	+ 0.5	+ 1.6	+ 4.8	+ 3.2
	4	− 2.1	+ 1.9	+ 2.0	+ 6.2	+ 4.1
1978	1	− 7.3	+ 10.6	+ 15.9	+ 14.8	+ 15.4
	2	+ 8.2	+ 10.4	+ 8.4	+ 6.4	+ 7.4
	3	+ 7.9	+ 14.7	+ 12.7	+ 11.0	+ 11.9
	4	− 4.0	− 6.9	− 4.9	− 2.6	− 3.8
1979	1	+ 4.4	+ 13.9	+ 11.9	+ 13.8	+ 12.8
	2	− 1.1	+ 8.4	+ 7.5	+ 12.6	+ 10.1
	3	+ 4.1	+ 8.5	+ 6.5	+ 8.6	+ 7.6
	4	− 2.6	+ 2.1	+ 2.7	+ 6.4	+ 4.5
1980	1	− 4.1	− 4.2	− 2.1	0	− 1.0
	2	+ 9.4	+ 15.7	+ 13.7	+ 10.6	+ 12.1
	3	+ 10.0	+ 11.2	+ 9.2	+ 5.4	+ 7.3
	4	+ 7.3	+ 7.2	+ 5.2	+ 4.2	+ 4.7
1981	1	− 0.7	+ 11.8	+ 9.8	+ 16.0	+ 12.9
	2	− 4.2	+ 1.5	+ 3.7	+ 5.8	+ 4.7
	3	− 11.5	− 12.1	− 2.6	− 7.8	− 5.2
	4	+ 3.2	+ 4.7	+ 2.7	+ 5.8	+ 4.2
1982	1	− 7.0	− 0.3	+ 4.7	+ 4.0	+ 4.3
	2	− 1.5	+ 2.2	+ 1.7	+ 6.4	+ 4.1
	3	+ 9.8	+ 8.8	+ 6.8	+ 3.2	+ 5.0
	4	+ 18.2	+ 18.0	+ 16.0	+ 4.0	+ 10.0
1983	1	+ 8.2	+ 12.3	+ 10.3	+ 8.4	+ 9.3
	2	+ 9.6	+ 20.0	+ 18.0	+ 14.6	+ 16.3
	3	− 0.9	− 7.6	− 8.7	− 3.4	− 6.0
	4	− 0.6	− 1.4	− 2.8	+ 2.8	0
1984	1	− 5.6	+ 1.2	+ 4.8	+ 5.4	+ 5.1
	2	− 3.1	− 7.2	− 6.1	− 3.0	− 4.5
	3	+ 8.8	+ 4.2	+ 2.2	− 0.4	+ 0.9
	4	− 0.1	+ 1.1	− 0.8	+ 5.4	+ 2.3

Calls = 4.25%, puts = 2.0%

Table 10-2. The Noddings-Calamos aggressive convertible bond index and hedging strategies using *undervalued* S&P 100 index puts and/or overpriced calls—1976–84

Year	S&P 500	Aggressive convertible bond index	Strategy 33 long puts	Strategy 34 short calls	Strategy 35 puts & calls
1976	+ 23.6%	+ 33.1%	+ 23.4%	+ 33.9%	+ 28.8%
1977	− 7.2	+ 9.0	+ 15.9	+ 26.5	+ 21.2
1978	+ 6.6	+ 30.4	+ 34.6	+ 32.1	+ 33.4
1979	+ 18.4	+ 36.8	+ 31.6	+ 48.1	+ 39.6
1980	+ 32.5	+ 32.1	+ 27.9	+ 21.5	+ 24.7
1981	− 5.0	+ 4.4	+ 13.9	+ 19.7	+ 16.8
1982	+ 21.6	+ 30.8	+ 31.9	+ 18.8	+ 25.4
1983	+ 22.5	+ 22.8	+ 15.5	+ 23.4	+ 19.5
1984	+ 6.2	− 1.1	− 0.2	+ 7.3	+ 3.6

Last 5-year data					
Cumulative return		119%	121%	129%	126%
Annualized return		17.0	17.2	18.0	17.7
Average quarterly return		4.4	4.3	4.4	4.3
Standard deviation		8.8	7.1	5.7	6.0
Coefficient of variation		201	166	130	139

9-year data					
Cumulative return		467%	461%	658%	557%
Annualized return		21.3	21.1	25.2	23.3
Average quarterly return		5.2	5.1	5.9	5.5
Standard deviation		7.5	6.3	5.5	5.5
Coefficient of variation		144	123	92	99

Calls = 4.25%, puts = 2.0%

risk-reward relationships were nearly identical for the last five years. However, the annualized returns for aggressive convertibles and their related SuperHedges averaged about 4 percent higher over the full nine-year period. The study's initial four years saw low-cap common stocks produce phenomenal results.

Looking at the quarterly calculations of Table 10-1, we can again see divergences similar to those of the low-risk convertible SuperHedges of Chapter 9. Most negative performance variations occurred in the last six quarters, a period when the aggressive index was made up mostly of AMEX and over-the-counter issues (in the earlier years most were NYSE-listed). The S&P 100 would not have been the most appropriate index for aggressive convertible bonds during that time period. More representative index options might have been those on the Amex Market Value Index or the Value Line Composite Index. I will evaluate both.

HEDGING AGGRESSIVE CONVERTIBLES WITH INEFFICIENTLY PRICED AMEX INDEX OPTIONS

Although few portfolios would be expected to mirror the American Stock Exchange's speculative stocks, its index options can be useful tools for controlling risk. AMEX puts and calls used in combination with those on a high-quality index such as the S&P 100 may help fine tune the risk-reward characteristics of hedged portfolios that include secondary securities.

The calculations of Chapter 8 assume normal values for three-month AMEX puts and calls at 3.5 and 6 percent. The quarterly calculations of Table 10-3 pit them against the aggressive convertible bond index and assume modestly undervalued puts at 3 percent and modestly overpriced calls at 6.5 percent. As shown by the performance summaries of Table 10-4, AMEX options enhanced returns over the last five years of the study but performed poorly during the early years when low-priced energy stocks soared. The worst divergence occurred in 1979, when the AMEX index advanced 64.4 percent. Selling AMEX calls would have reduced the convertible portfolio's best-year 36.8 percent gain down to a meager 3.7 percent—the sale of S&P 100 calls that same year would have produced a spectacular 48.1 percent return (Table 10-2).

Unless a portfolio can be expected to respond in tandem with a major upward move in secondary stocks, I would avoid selling AMEX calls. However, I would not hesitate to use the AMEX puts for protecting aggressive convertible bonds, especially if they could be purchased at bargain prices. When buying puts, one is always dealing with a known risk, the premium paid. The sale of index calls, however, presents unlimited upside risk.

HEDGING AGGRESSIVE CONVERTIBLES WITH INEFFICIENTLY PRICED VALUE LINE INDEX OPTIONS

Covering 1,700 stocks, the unweighted Value Line Composite Index may be the best measurement standard for most portfolios of common stocks or

Table 10-3. Quarterly returns for the Noddings-Calamos aggressive convertible bond if hedged by three-month AMEX at-the-money, *undervalued* index puts and/or *overpriced* calls—1976–84

Year	Quarter	AMEX	Aggressive convertible bond index	Strategy 33a long puts	Strategy 34a short calls	Strategy 35a puts & calls
1976	1	+ 24.9%	+ 9.7%	+ 6.7%	− 8.7%	− 1.0%
	2	+ 1.0	+ 9.0	+ 6.0	+ 14.5	+ 10.2
	3	− 3.2	+ 6.1	+ 6.3	+ 12.6	+ 9.4
	4	+ 7.7	+ 4.9	+ 1.9	+ 3.7	+ 2.8
1977	1	+ 1.2	+ 1.5	− 1.5	+ 6.8	+ 2.6
	2	+ 8.2	+ 4.9	+ 1.9	+ 3.2	+ 2.6
	3	− 1.2	+ 0.5	− 1.3	+ 7.0	+ 2.8
	4	+ 7.6	+ 1.9	− 1.1	+ 0.8	− 0.2
1978	1	+ 0.8	+ 10.6	+ 7.6	+ 16.3	+ 12.0
	2	+ 12.9	+ 10.4	+ 7.4	+ 4.0	+ 5.7
	3	+ 16.0	+ 14.7	+ 11.7	+ 5.2	+ 8.4
	4	− 10.8	− 6.9	+ 0.9	− 0.4	+ 0.2
1979	1	+ 19.4	+ 13.9	+ 10.9	+ 1.0	+ 6.0
	2	+ 11.7	+ 8.4	+ 5.4	+ 3.2	+ 4.3
	3	+ 2.2	+ 8.5	+ 5.5	+ 12.8	+ 9.2
	4	+ 20.4	+ 2.1	− 0.9	− 11.8	− 6.4
1980	1	− 5.7	− 4.2	− 1.5	+ 2.3	+ 0.4
	2	+ 26.0	+ 15.7	+ 12.7	− 3.8	+ 4.4
	3	+ 12.9	+ 11.2	+ 8.2	+ 4.8	+ 6.5
	4	+ 5.3	+ 7.2	+ 4.2	+ 8.4	+ 6.3
1981	1	+ 3.3	+ 11.8	+ 8.8	+ 15.0	+ 11.9
	2	+ 3.9	+ 1.5	− 1.5	+ 4.1	+ 1.3
	3	− 21.8	− 12.1	+ 6.7	− 5.6	+ 0.6
	4	+ 9.5	+ 4.7	+ 1.7	+ 1.7	+ 1.7
1982	1	− 18.9	− 0.3	+ 15.6	+ 6.2	+ 10.9
	2	− 3.6	+ 2.2	+ 2.8	+ 8.7	+ 5.8
	3	+ 12.9	+ 8.8	+ 5.8	+ 2.4	+ 4.1
	4	+ 20.3	+ 18.0	+ 15.0	+ 4.2	+ 9.6
1983	1	+ 14.2	+ 12.3	+ 9.3	+ 4.6	+ 7.0
	2	+ 24.6	+ 20.0	+ 17.0	+ 1.9	+ 9.4
	3	− 5.0	− 7.6	− 5.6	− 1.1	− 3.4
	4	− 3.1	− 1.4	− 1.3	+ 5.1	+ 1.9
1984	1	− 5.4	+ 1.2	+ 3.6	+ 7.7	+ 5.6
	2	− 5.1	− 7.2	− 5.1	− 0.7	− 2.9
	3	+ 7.6	+ 4.2	+ 1.2	+ 3.1	+ 2.2
	4	− 5.2	+ 1.1	+ 3.3	+ 7.6	+ 5.4

Calls = 6.5%, puts = 3.0%

Table 10-4. The Noddings-Calamos aggressive convertible bond index and hedging strategies using *undervalued* AMEX index puts and/or *overpriced* calls—1976-84

Year	AMEX	Aggressive convertible bond index	Strategy 33a long puts	Strategy 34a short calls	Strategy 35a puts & calls
1976	+ 31.6%	+ 33.1%	+ 22.5%	+ 22.1%	+ 22.7%
1977	+ 16.4	+ 9.0	− 2.0	+ 18.9	+ 8.0
1978	+ 17.7	+ 30.4	+ 30.2	+ 26.7	+ 28.6
1979	+ 64.4	+ 36.8	+ 22.2	+ 3.7	+ 13.0
1980	+ 41.2	+ 32.1	+ 25.2	+ 11.8	+ 18.7
1981	− 8.1	+ 4.4	+ 16.3	+ 14.9	+ 16.0
1982	+ 6.2	+ 30.8	+ 44.6	+ 23.2	+ 33.9
1983	+ 31.0	+ 22.8	+ 19.2	+ 10.8	+ 15.2
1984	− 8.4	− 1.1	+ 2.8	+ 18.6	+ 9.9

Last 5-year data

Cumulative return		119%	158%	108%	133%
Annualized return		17.0	20.9	15.8	18.4
Average quarterly return		4.4	5.0	3.8	4.4
Standard deviation		8.8	6.6	4.7	4.2
Coefficient of variation		201	132	122	96

9-year data

Cumulative return		467%	392%	297%	351%
Annualized return		21.3	19.4	16.6	18.2
Average quarterly return		5.2	4.7	4.1	4.4
Standard deviation		7.5	5.7	6.1	4.5
Coefficient of variation		144	121	149	102

Calls = 6.5%, puts = 3.0%

convertibles. Its index puts and calls should receive serious attention by all hedge investors.

Yielding about 1 percent less than the S&P 100, the Value Line put-call price spread for three-month options should be about 1.5 percent when Treasury bills are at 10 percent, compared to 1.25 percent for the S&P 100. Keeping in mind Value Line's higher price volatility than the S&P, normal put and call premiums are assumed to be 3 and 4.5 percent respectively, versus 2.5 and 3.75 percent for the S&P and 3.5 and 6 percent for the AMEX.

As with the previous SuperHedge calculations, the quarterly returns of Table 10-5 are based on modestly undervalued puts at 2.5 percent and modestly

Table 10-5. Quarterly returns for the Noddings-Calamos aggressive convertible bond index if hedged by three-month Value Line at-the-money, *undervalued* index puts and/or *overpriced* calls—1976–84

Year	Quarter	Value Line	Aggressive convertible bond index	Strategy 33b long puts	Strategy 34b short calls	Strategy 35b puts & calls
1976	1	+ 25.0%	+ 9.7%	+ 7.2%	− 10.3%	− 1.6%
	2	− 0.6	+ 9.0	+ 7.1	+ 14.0	+ 10.6
	3	− 1.2	+ 6.1	+ 4.8	+ 11.1	+ 8.0
	4	+ 7.7	+ 4.9	+ 2.4	+ 2.2	+ 2.3
1977	1	− 3.3	+ 1.5	+ 2.3	+ 6.5	+ 4.4
	2	+ 5.0	+ 4.9	+ 2.4	+ 4.9	+ 3.6
	3	− 3.9	+ 0.5	+ 1.9	+ 5.5	+ 3.7
	4	+ 3.0	+ 1.9	− 0.6	+ 3.9	+ 1.6
1978	1	+ 1.1	+ 10.6	+ 8.1	+ 14.5	+ 11.3
	2	+ 9.7	+ 10.4	+ 7.9	+ 5.7	+ 6.8
	3	+ 9.9	+ 14.7	+ 12.2	+ 9.8	+ 11.0
	4	− 14.4	− 6.9	+ 5.0	− 1.9	+ 1.6
1979	1	+ 11.7	+ 13.9	+ 11.4	+ 7.2	+ 9.3
	2	+ 4.2	+ 8.4	+ 5.9	+ 9.2	+ 7.6
	3	+ 8.0	+ 8.5	+ 6.0	+ 5.5	+ 5.8
	4	− 1.0	+ 2.1	+ 0.6	+ 7.1	+ 3.8
1980	1	− 12.9	− 4.2	+ 6.2	+ 0.8	+ 3.5
	2	+ 16.5	+ 15.7	+ 13.2	+ 4.2	+ 8.7
	3	+ 14.2	+ 11.2	+ 8.7	+ 2.0	+ 5.4
	4	+ 2.1	+ 7.2	+ 4.7	+ 10.1	+ 7.4
1981	1	+ 5.7	+ 11.8	+ 9.3	+ 11.1	+ 10.2
	2	+ 1.7	+ 1.5	− 1.0	+ 4.8	+ 1.9
	3	− 16.3	− 12.1	+ 1.7	− 7.1	− 2.7
	4	+ 6.2	+ 4.7	+ 2.2	+ 3.5	+ 2.8
1982	1	− 9.1	− 0.3	+ 6.3	+ 4.7	+ 5.5
	2	− 3.8	+ 2.2	+ 3.5	+ 7.2	+ 5.4
	3	+ 9.4	+ 8.8	+ 6.3	+ 4.4	+ 5.4
	4	+ 20.5	+ 18.0	+ 15.5	+ 2.5	+ 9.0
1983	1	+ 12.8	+ 12.3	+ 9.8	+ 4.5	+ 7.2
	2	+ 14.2	+ 20.0	+ 17.5	+ 10.8	+ 14.2
	3	− 2.7	− 7.6	− 7.4	− 2.6	− 5.0
	4	− 2.4	− 1.4	− 1.5	+ 3.6	+ 1.0
1984	1	− 6.3	+ 1.2	+ 5.0	+ 6.2	+ 5.6
	2	− 5.2	− 7.2	− 4.5	− 2.2	− 3.4
	3	+ 5.6	+ 4.2	+ 1.7	+ 3.6	+ 2.6
	4	− 2.8	+ 1.1	+ 1.4	+ 6.1	+ 3.8

Calls = 5.0%, puts = 2.5%

Table 10-6. The Noddings-Calamos aggressive convertible bond index and hedging strategies using *undervalued* Value Line index puts and/or *overpriced* calls—1976—84

Year	Value Line*	Aggressive convertible bond index	Strategy 33b long puts	Strategy 34b short calls	Strategy 35b puts & calls
1976	+ 33.2%	+ 33.1%	+ 23.2%	+ 16.1%	+ 20.2%
1977	+ 0.5	+ 9.0	+ 6.1	+ 22.5	+ 14.0
1978	+ 4.3	+ 30.4	+ 37.4	+ 30.4	+ 34.1
1979	+ 29.8	+ 36.8	+ 25.8	+ 32.3	+ 29.2
1980	+ 18.3	+ 32.1	+ 36.8	+ 18.0	+ 27.4
1981	- 4.4	+ 4.4	+ 12.5	+ 12.0	+ 12.3
1982	+ 15.3	+ 30.8	+ 35.1	+ 20.1	+ 27.8
1983	+ 22.3	+ 22.8	+ 17.7	+ 16.8	+ 17.5
1984	- 8.8	- 1.1	+ 3.4	+ 14.2	+ 8.6

Last 5-year data				
Cumulative return	119%	155%	112%	133%
Annualized return	17.0	20.6	16.2	18.4
Average quarterly return	4.4	4.9	3.9	4.4
Standard deviation	8.8	6.3	4.5	4.7
Coefficient of variation	201	128	114	106

9-year data				
Cumulative return	467%	477%	419%	453%
Annualized return	21.3	21.5	20.1	20.9
Average quarterly return	5.2	5.1	4.8	5.0
Standard deviation	7.5	5.2	5.2	4.3
Coeffficient of variation	144		108	87

*Excludes dividends averaging about 3-4 percent annually.
Calls = 5.0%, puts = 2.5%

overpriced calls at 5 percent. From Table 10-6, it can be seen that Value Line options would have produced very satisfactory hedge returns over both the five- and nine-year periods, with fewer divergences than experienced with the AMEX options. Exhibits 10-1 and 10-2 show above-the-line performance for all three hedge strategies.

The tables and exhibits show Value Line put hedges outperforming call hedges. Perhaps this might indicate that my premium assumptions are too low; however, actual market prices have been running below my 3 and 4.5 percent normal-premium assumptions. Since call premiums on the S&P 100 have been

Exhibit 10-1. Risk-reward analysis for aggressive convertible bond strategies using inefficiently priced Value Line index options, 5 years (1980–84)

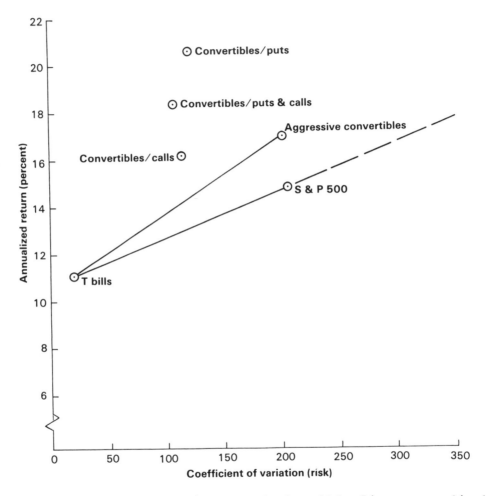

trading closer to their theoretical normal values, Value Line puts combined with S&P 100 calls might be the best strategy for investors wanting to fabricate a short sale on the market.

SuperHedgers should actively search for the best opportunities when making actual purchases or sales—they shouldn't arbitrarily select the popular S&P 100s simply because they offer better trading liquidity. Remember that bargains, as with convertible securities, are usually found in areas out of the market's

Exhibit 10-2. Risk-reward analysis for aggressive convertible bond strategies using inefficiently priced Value Line options, 9 years (1976–84)

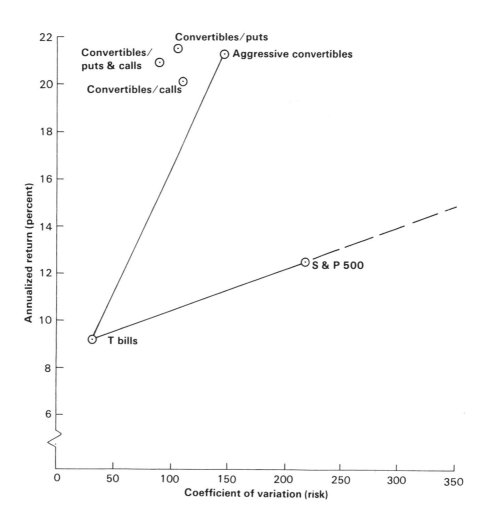

mainstream. Using May 1985 (when this chapter was written) as an example, December 195 puts on the Value Line Index were available at a bargain-basement price of $3.50. With an index market value of 197, the seven-month, slightly-out-of-the-money puts were trading at a premium of only 1.8 percent, less than my normal-value assumption for the shorter-term three-month puts.

SOME FINAL THOUGHTS

The question is often raised about the possibility of all financial markets ultimately becoming efficient. In that scenario, the kinds of attractive situations you have learned about would cease to exist. I don't believe that will happen. I have been hedging convertibles for nearly twenty years, and although strategies change from time to time, the opportunities are greater now than they were when I first started. Further, they accommodate larger sums of money and permit broader portfolio diversification.

All investors, large or small, can use the traditional hedge strategies of Chapters 6 and 7. However, a realistic minimum for building a diversified SuperHedge portfolio is about $250,000. This amount assures adequate diversification (about twenty-five different issues) when purchasing either low-risk or aggressive convertibles in ten-bond unit sizes. Smaller investors, however, may also SuperHedge by using the closed-end or mutual funds that specialize in convertible securities for the long side of their hedge portfolios (Chapter 5 and Appendix E). When looking at a fund, study its portfolio carefully so that the most appropriate index options may be selected—most funds will have a mixture of both low-risk and aggressive issues. Also make sure that the fund itself is not using options to avoid hedging its portfolio twice. If it is using hedging strategies, don't necessarily reject it. The fund can probably execute the strategies at lower costs that individual investors are able to.

I must again emphasize my strong belief that investing is a long-term activity. No investment strategy should be entered into with a time horizon of less than five years. However, do not be surprised if profitable workouts occur faster than expected. When we first employed SuperHedging using the discounted dual-purpose funds (1975), for instance, we were fully prepared to hold them until final termination dates (up to ten years in 1985). We could not foresee that their discounts would nearly vanish in about three years. Be prepared to shift strategies as better opportunities unfold. As the dual-purpose funds' discounts dwindled, for example, undervalued convertible securities presented more favorable risk-reward trade-offs and became the new core holdings for superhedge strategies. As it became harder to find inefficiently priced options, we temporarily backed away from hedging with unrelated options and returned to the tried-and-true traditional hedging strategies of Chapters 6 and 7.

There is no finer investment strategy than dealing with market inefficiencies. However, the unconventional strategies you have just studied will probably never be recommended by your accountant, attorney, banker, or other advisors. Skilled in their own professions, they cannot be expected to be experts in financial strategies, especially those out of the mainstream. You must become your own expert. You will probably feel quite alone at times, but that's the price you must pay for doing anything nontraditional. Highly profitable investments are always nontraditional.

Possible Tax Effects of Various Option Strategies

The source for this appendix is a booklet titled *Taxes and Investing* prepared by Oppenheim, Appel, Dixon & Co., Certified Public Accountants, at the request of the New York Stock Exchange Inc. (1984). The opinions and conclusions expressed are those of Oppenheim, Appel, Dixon & Co.

In the absence of even proposed regulations on offsetting positions, the following chart represents the current opinion of Oppenheim, Appel, Dixon & Co. as to the appropriate treatment of the described transactions for federal income tax purposes. Regulations may be issued by the Internal Revenue Service in the future which may result in tax treatment contrary to the conclusions set forth below. Investors are advised to consult their tax and legal advisors in considering the tax consequences of their own specific circumstances.

Positions	Effect on holding period	Defferal of loss[1]	Capitalization of interest and carrying charges
1. *LONG STOCK—SHORT STOCK* (substantially identical)			
a. *Long Stock*: gain position *Time of short sale*: stock long-term	No effect[2]	No	No

b. *Long stock*: gain position *Time of short sale*: stock held short-term or prior to acquisition of stock	Terminate	No	No
c. *Long stock*: loss position *Time of short sale*: stock held long-term	(See footnote 2)	No	No
d. *Long stock*: loss position *Time of short sale*: stock held short-term or prior to acquisition of stock	Terminate	No	No
2. *LONG STOCK—SHORT* STOCK (not substantially identical)	No effect	No	No
3. *LONG STOCK—SHORT CALL* (not qualified call)	Terminate[3]	Yes	Yes
4. *LONG STOCK—SHORT* *OUT-OF-THE-MONEY* *QUALIFIED COVERED CALL*			
a. *Long stock*: gain or loss position *Time of writing call*: not relevant *Call closed*: same year as stock disposed, gain or loss on call not relevant	No effect	No	No
b. *Long stock*: gain position *Time of writing call*: not relevant *Call closed*: at loss, year preceeding disposition of stock *Days stock held after call closed*: less than thirty days[4]	No effect	Yes	No
c. *Long stock*: gain position *Time of writing call*: not relevant *Call closed*: at loss, year preceeding disposition of stock	No effect	No	No

Days stock held after call closed: thirty days or more[4]			
d. *Long stock*: loss position *Time of writing call*: not relevant *Call closed*: at gain, year preceding disposition of stock *Days stock held after call closed*: not relevant	No effect	Not applicable	No

5. *LONG STOCK—SHORT IN-THE-MONEY QUALIFIED COVERED CALL*

a. *Long stock*: gain or loss position *Time of writing call*: stock held long-term *Call closed*: same year as stock disposed, gain or loss on call not relevant	No effect[2]	No	No
b. *Long stock*: gain or loss position *Time of writing call*: stock held short-term *Call closed*: same year as stock disposed, gain or loss on call not relevant	Suspend	No	No No
c. *Long stock*: gain position *Time of writing call*: stock held long-term *Call closed*: at loss, year preceding disposition of stock *Days stock held after call closed*: less than thirty days[4]	No effect[2]	Yes	No
d. *Long stock*: gain position *Time of writing call*: stock held long-term *Call closed*: at loss, year preceding disposition of stock	No effect[2]	No	No

Days stock held after call closed: Thirty days or more[4]			
e. *Long stock*: gain position *Time of writing call*: stock held short-term *Call closed*: at loss, year preceding disposition of stock *Days stock held after call closed*: less than thirty days[4]	Suspend	Yes	No
f. *Long stock*: gain position *Time of writing call*: stock held short-term *Call closed*: at loss, year preceding disposition of stock *Days stock held after call closed*: Thirty days or more[4]	Suspend	No	No
g. *Long stock*: loss position *Time of writing call*: stock held short-term *Call closed*: at gain, year preceding disposition of stock *Days stock held after call closed*: not relevant	Suspend	Not applicable	No
h. *Long stock*: loss position *Time of writing call*: stock held long-term *Call closed*: at gain, year preceding disposition of stock *Days stock held after call closed*: not relevant	No effect	Not applicable	No
6. *LONG STOCK—SHORT PUT*	No effect	No	No
7. *SHORT STOCK—SHORT PUT*	Not appl.	Yes[5]	Yes[5]
8. *LONG CALL—SHORT CALL*	Terminate	Yes	Yes
9. *LONG CALL—LONG PUT*	Terminate	Yes	Yes
10. *LONG CALL—SHORT STOCK*	Terminate	Yes	Yes
11. *LONG CALL—SHORT PUT*	Terminate[5]	Yes[5]	Yes[5]
12. *LONG PUT—SHORT CALL*	Terminate[5]	Yes[5]	Yes[5]

13. *SHORT CALL—SHORT PUT*	Not appl.	Yes[5]	Yes[5]
14. *LONG PUT—SHORT STOCK*	No effect	No	No
15. *LONG STOCK—LONG PUT* ("married put")	No effect	No	No
16. *LONG STOCK—LONG PUT* (not "married put" or "divorced" married put)			
a. *Stock held*: short-term	Terminate	Yes	Yes
b. *Stock held*: long-term	No effect[6]	Yes	Yes

[1] When there are offsetting positions in a straddle, losses realized on the closing of a position in one year are deferred to the extent of the unrecognized gain on another positon. The deferred loss is properly recognized by the taxpayer in a subsequent year.

[2] Any loss on closing the short sale or the call, as the case may be, will be deemed to be a long-term capital loss, regardless of when recognized.

[3] If the stock is held long-term at the time the call is written, the rule of footnote 2 should apply.

[4] According to the Conference Report to the Deficit Reduction Act of 1984, only days on which the stock is held with no offsetting position will generally be counted.

[5] This is based on the assumption that the premium received constitutes a substantial reduction of risk. That may not, however, be the case. If there is no substantial reduction of risk, these would not be offsetting positions, and the anti-straddle rules would not apply.

[6] Loss on the put will be long-term regardless of holding period.

Stocks With Listed Put and Call Options, April 1985

Company	Stock Volatility	Stock Yield
AMF	100%	2.8%
AMR	135	0
ASA Limited	115	3.8
Abbott Labs	80	2.6
Advanced Micro Devices	145	0
Aetna Life & Casualty	75	6.4
Air Products & Chemicals	95	2.5
Alexander & Alexander	105	3.3
Allied Corp.	80	4.7
Allied Stores	80	3.8

Company	Stock Volatility	Stock Yield
Allis-Chalmers	130	0
Aluminum Co. America	90	3.5
AMAX	120	1.1
Amdahl	150	1.3
Amerada Hess	125	3.4
American Brands	60	5.6
American Broadcasting	95	1.5
American Can	80	5.4
American Cyanamid	95	3.6
American Electric Power	50	10.9
American Express	100	3.0
American Home Products	60	4.7
American Hospital Supply	85	3.3
American International Group	80	0.6
American Medical International	120	2.8
American Telephone & Telegraph	85	5.5
AMP	90	2.2
Anheuser-Busch Cos.	70	2.5
Apache	135	2.4
Archer Daniels Midland	105	0.7
Arkla	110	5.1
Armco	95	0
ASARCO	130	0
Ashland Oil	105	5.5
Atlantic Richfield	95	6.1
Automatic Data Processing	85	1.4
Avnet	105	1.5
Avon Products	80	9.6
Baker International	120	5.5
Bally Manufacturing	115	1.3
BankAmerica	85	8.1
Bard (C.R.)	105	1.6
Bausch & Lomb	90	2.9
Baxter Travenol Labs	85	2.3
Beatrice Companies	70	5.9

Company	Stock Volatility	Stock Yield
Becton Dickinson & Co.	65	2.4
BellSouth	80	7.9
Bethlehem Steel	100	2.2
Beverly Enterprises	120	0.9
Black & Decker Manufacturing	95	3.0
Boeing Co.	100	2.2
Boise Cascade	90	5.0
Bristol-Meyers Co.	70	3.2
Browning Ferris	100	2.4
Brunswick	125	2.7
Bucyrus Erie	100	3.0
Burlington Northern	100	2.7
Burroughs	85	4.3
CBS Inc.	80	2.8
CIGNA Corp.	90	5.2
CSX Corp.	90	4.3
Capital Cities Communications	75	0.1
Carter Hawley Hale	110	4.5
Caterpillar Tractor	90	1.5
Celanese	75	4.7
Cessna Aircraft	125	2.1
Champion International	100	1.9
Chase Manhattan Corp.	85	7.3
Chevron	95	7.3
Chemical New York Corp.	80	6.6
Chevron	90	6.9
Chicago & Northwest Transportation	145	0
Chrysler	145	2.8
Church's Fried Chicken	90	2.1
Cincinnati Milacron	105	3.1
Citicorp	95	5.3
City Investing	100	0
Clorox	100	3.5
Coastal Corp.	135	0.9
Coca-Cola	65	4.2

Company	Stock Volatility	Stock Yield
Coleco Industries	190	0
Colgate Palmolive	75	5.2
Colt Industries	100	4.3
Combustion Engineering	100	5.3
Comdisco	165	1.3
Commodore International	180	0
Commonwealth Edison	60	10.1
Communications Satellite	100	3.9
Community Psychiatric Centers	120	0.7
Computer Sciences	120	0
Computervision	140	0
Consolidated Edison	60	7.4
Continental Telecommunications	60	7.5
Control Data	110	2.4
Cooper Industries	105	5.2
CooperVision	150	1.8
Corning Glass Works	80	3.6
Cray Research	140	0
Crown Zellerbach	100	2.4
Cullinet Software	130	0
Dart & Kraft	55	4.6
Data General	145	0
Datapoint	165	0
Dataproducts	150	1.2
Dayton Hudson	90	1.9
Deere & Co.	90	3.3
Delta Air Lines	110	1.7
Diamond Shamrock	100	9.1
Diebold	100	1.9
Digital Equipment	105	0
Disney (Walt) Productions	95	1.6
Dominion Resources	55	9.2
Dow Chemical	85	6.3
Dresser Industries	110	3.8
du Pont (E.I.)	80	5.7

Company	Stock Volatility	Stock Yield
Duke Power	55	7.5
Dun & Bradstreet	70	2.6
EG&G	100	1.3
E-Systems	110	1.8
Eastern Gas & Fuel	100	5.5
Eastman Kodak	60	5.4
Eckerd (Jack)	90	3.6
Edwards (A.G.)	130	2.6
Emerson Electric	65	3.7
Emery Air Freight	125	2.9
Engelhard	100	2.4
ENSERCH	100	5.5
Exxon	60	6.8
Federal Express	120	0
Federal National Mortgage Assn.	135	1.0
Financial Corp. America	200	0
Firestone Tire & Rubber	95	4.4
First Boston	120	3.8
First Chicago	105	6.1
First Mississippi	140	2.3
Fleetwood Enterprises	135	1.7
Fluor	115	2.1
Ford Motor	105	5.8
Foster Wheeler	115	3.1
Freeport-McMoran	125	2.8
GAF	115	0.7
GCA	160	0
GTE	65	7.6
General Dynamics	110	1.4
General Electric	65	3.7
General Foods	60	4.1
General Instrument	125	3.0
General Motors	80	6.8
GenRad	160	0.6
Genuine Parts	80	3.6

Company	Stock Volatility	Stock Yield
GEO International	150	0
Georgia Pacific	100	3.7
Gerber Scientific	175	0.6
Gillette	70	4.5
Global Marine	150	5.3
Golden Nugget	130	0
Golden West Financial	155	0.7
Goodyear Tire & Rubber	85	5.7
Gould	110	2.9
Grace (W.R.) & Co.	70	6.7
Great Western Financial	135	3.2
Greyhound	85	4.4
Gulf & Western Industries	90	3.3
Hall (Frank B.) & Co.	95	4.1
Halliburton	110	5.8
Harris Corp.	100	3.1
Hecla Mining	150	1.2
Hercules	95	4.8
Hewlett-Packard	95	0.6
Hilton Hotels	85	2.8
Hitachi Ltd. ADR	95	0.6
Holiday Inns	100	1.9
Homestake Mining	125	0.8
Honeywell	90	3.2
Hospital Corp. of America	100	1.4
Household International	85	4.8
Houston Natural Gas	95	4.5
Hughes Tool	120	3.2
Humana	110	2.3
Hutton (E.F.) Group	145	2.1
ITT	110	2.8
Inexco Oil	140	2.0
International Business Machines	65	3.4
International Flavors & Fragrances	90	3.9
International Minerals & Chemicals	95	6.3

Company	Stock Volatility	Stock Yield
International Paper	80	4.8
Johnson & Johnson	75	2.9
Joy Manufacturing	85	5.5
K mart	100	3.7
Kaneb Services	120	4.0
Kerr McGee	105	3.5
Key Pharmaceuticals	145	2.0
LTV	135	0
Lear Siegler	95	3.7
Lehman Corp.	65	11.0
Levi Strauss & Co.	110	5.6
Lilly (Eli) & Co.	65	4.1
Limited Inc.	130	0.8
Litton Industries	95	2.9
Lockheed	120	1.2
Loews	80	2.3
Loral	105	1.6
Louisiana Land & Exploration	120	2.9
Louisiana-Pacific	105	3.9
M/A-COM	150	1.2
MCA	85	1.8
MGM/UA Entertainment	150	5.6
Macy (R.H.)	90	2.6
Manufacturers Hanover	90	8.9
MAPCO	95	3.2
Marriott	85	0.6
Martin Marietta	115	3.0
Mary Kay Cosmetics	145	1.0
McDermott International	110	7.0
McDonalds	75	1.4
McDonnell Douglas	105	2.4
Medtronic	100	2.5
Merck & Co.	60	3.1
Merill Lynch & Co.	140	2.5
Mesa Petroleum	135	1.0

Company	Stock Volatility	Stock Yield
Middle South Utilities	70	13.1
Minnesota Mining & Manufacturing	65	4.2
Mitchell Energy & Development	140	1.6
Mobil	95	7.5
Mohawk Data Sciences	140	0
Monsanto	80	5.3
Morgan (J.P.) & Co.	70	4.8
Motorola	95	1.9
Murphy Oil	135	3.3
NBI	140	0
NCR	100	3.1
NL Industries	120	1.7
NWA	110	2.2
National Distillers & Chemical	65	7.2
National Medical Enterprises	115	1.9
National Patent Development	155	0.6
National Semiconductor	140	0
Newmont Mining	120	2.3
Noble Affiliates	135	0.8
Norfolk Southern	75	5.2
Northrop	105	2.8
Northwest Industries	110	4.9
Novo Industri A/S ADR	115	0.8
Occidental Petroleum	90	8.4
Ocean Drilling & Exploration	135	3.8
Owens-Corning Fiberglas	115	4.3
Owens-Illinois	80	4.0
PPG Industries	85	4.3
Paine Webber Group	165	1.5
Panhandle Eastern	95	6.1
Paradyne	155	0
Parker Drilling	140	2.5
Penn Central	115	0
Penny (J.C.)	95	4.9
Pennzoil	110	4.6

Company	Stock Volatility	Stock Yield
PepsiCo	80	3.1
Perkin-Elmer	120	2.2
Pfizer	75	3.4
Phelps Dodge	120	0
Philbro-Salomon	140	1.4
Philip Morris	65	4.3
Phillips Petroleum	110	6.3
Pillsbury	75	3.2
Pioneer Corp.	125	4.1
Pitney-Bowes	90	3.1
Pittston	110	0
Pogo Producing	120	3.4
Polaroid	100	3.3
Prime Computer	155	0
Procter & Gamble	55	4.8
Pulte Home	145	0.8
Quaker Oats	70	2.8
RCA	90	2.5
Ralston Purina	80	2.4
Raychem	105	0.7
Raytheon	90	3.5
Reading & Bates	140	4.3
Resorts International	125	0
Revco Drug Stores	105	3.2
Revlon	95	5.0
Reynolds (R.J.) Industries	70	3.9
Reynolds Metals	85	2.7
Rockwell International	105	2.8
Rowan Companies	130	0.9
Royal Dutch Petroleum	80	4.9
Ryder System	90	2.4
Sabine	120	0.2
Safeway Stores	75	4.9
Sanders Associates	105	1.5
Santa Fe Southern Pacific	95	3.6

Company	Stock Volatility	Stock Yield
Schering-Plough	70	4.1
Schlumberger	100	3.1
Scientific-Atlanta	130	1.1
Scott Paper	85	3.1
Sea-Land	105	2.4
Searle (G.D.) & Co.	100	2.0
Sears Roebuck & Co.	85	5.1
Security Pacific	80	4.4
SEDCO	130	1.3
Shaklee	135	5.4
Shell Oil	110	3.4
Signal Companies	105	3.0
Singer Co.	120	0.3
Skyline	110	3.2
Smith International	125	2.7
SmithKline Beckman	75	4.4
Sony Corp. ADR	110	0.9
Southern Co.	55	9.6
Southland	100	3.1
Southland Royalty Co.	140	0.8
Southwest Airlines	125	0.5
Sperry	95	3.6
Squibb	85	2.8
Standard Oil Co. Indiana	95	5.4
Standard Oil Ohio	105	5.9
Sterling Drug	85	3.7
Storage Technology	200	0
Storer Communications	100	0.5
Sun Co.	110	4.6
Sybron	90	5.6
Syntex	85	3.3
TIE/communications	190	0
TRW	75	3.8
Tandy	120	0
Tektronix	95	1.7

Company	Stock Volatility	Stock Yield
Teledyne	100	0
Telex	145	0
Tenneco	80	6.8
Teradyne	135	0
Tesoro Petroleum	130	3.2
Texaco	70	8.4
Texas Instruments	120	1.8
Texas Oil & Gas	115	1.0
Textron	95	4.0
Thrifty Corp.	110	2.9
Tidewater	130	4.7
Time	95	1.8
Toys R Us	110	0
Transamerica	80	5.8
Transworld	130	1.1
Travelers	90	5.0
Tri-Continental	60	3.9
UAL	130	2.2
Union Carbide	85	8.9
Union Pacific	105	3.6
USAir Group	120	0.4
United States Steel	90	3.7
United Technologies	80	3.5
Unocal	120	2.0
Upjohn	80	3.2
Valero Energy	150	0
Varian Associates	115	0.8
Veeco Instruments	135	2.0
Verbatim	170	0
Viacom International	115	1.0
Wal-Mart Stores	105	0.6
Walter (Jim)	105	4.1
Wang Labs	130	0.8
Warner Communications	125	0
Warner-Lambert	70	3.8

Company	Stock Volatility	Stock Yield
Waste Management	105	1.5
Wendy's International	110	1.2
Western Co. of North America	155	0
Western Union	130	0
Westinghouse Electric	85	3.3
Weyerhaeuser	90	4.6
Whittaker	120	2.6
Williams Companies	110	4.6
Winnebago Industries	165	0.6
Woolworth (F.W.)	85	4.2
Xerox	75	6.8
Zapata	140	5.8
Zenith Electronics	130	0

Source: Value Line Options

Convertibles on Stocks With Listed Options, April 1985

Company	Stock S&P	Convertible description	Conversion ratio[a]	End notes
Alexander & Alexander	B+	11.00 −07	25.641	
Allied Corp.	A−	$ 6.74 C	1.179	
Allied Corp.		$12.00 D	2.027	
Allied Corp.		7.75 −05	25.426	1
Allied Stores	A+	9.50 −07	25.000	
Allied Stores		8.75 −09	18.307	
Allis−Chalmers	C	$ 5.875 C	1.667	
AMAX	B−	$ 3.00	1.310	
Amerada Hess	B	$ 3.50	4.345	
American Brands	A+	$ 2.67	1.020	
American Can	B	$ 3.00	.868	
American International Group	A	$ 5.85 B	1.630	
American International Group		4.00 −97	36.630	
American Medical International	A	9.50 −01	41.017	
American Medical International		8.25 −08	25.00	

Company	Stock S&P	Convertible description	Conversion ratio[a]	End notes
Anheuser–Busch Cos.	A+	$ 3.60 A	.645	
Armco	C	$ 2.10	1.270	
Ashland Oil	B+	$ 3.96	1.000	
Atlantic Richfield	A	$ 3.00	6.800	
Atlantic Richfield		$ 2.80	2.400	
Automatic Data Processing	A	7.50 −01	17.479	
Avnet	B+	8.00 −13	19.231	
Bally Manufacturing	B	6.00 −98	34.494	
Bally Manufacturing		10.00 −06	30.599	
Bard (C.R.)	A+	4.25 −96	39.480	2
Baxter Travenol Labs	A	4.375−91	105.263	
Baxter Travenol Labs		4.75 −01	85.324	
Beatrice Companies	A+	$ 3.38 A	1.860	
Becton Dickinson & Co.	A	4.125−88	20.483	
Becton Dickinson & Co.		5.00 −89	15.408	
Becton Dickinson & Co.		10.75 −06	16.667	3
Bethlehem Steel	B−	$ 5.00 C	1.770	
Bethlehem Steel		$ 2.50	.840	
Beverly Enterprises	B+	7.625−03	24.425	
Boeing Co.	A−	8.875−06	23.669	
Boise Cascade	B+	$ 5.00 B	1.096	
Bristol–Myers Co.	A+	$ 2.00	2.120	
CIGNA Corp.	B+	$ 2.75 A	.422	
CSX Corp.	B+	$ 7.00 A	6.000	
Caterpillar Tractor	B	5.50 −00	19.802	
Celanese	B+	4.00 −90	10.870	
Celanese		9.75 −06	14.085	
Cessna Aircraft	B	8.00 −08	30.769	
Champion International	B	$ 1.20	1.000	
Champion International		$ 4.60	1.667	
Chase Manhattan Corp.	A−	4.875−93	18.182	4
Chase Manhattan Corp.		6.50− 96	17.391	
Chemical New York Corp.	A	$ 1.875	1.004	
Chemical New York Corp.		5.50 −96	31.696	
Chemical New York Corp.		5.00 −93	32.031	5

Company	Stock S&P	Convertible description	Conversion ratio[a]	End notes
Citicorp	A+	5.75 −00	24.390	
City Investing	A−	$ 2.00	1.561	
City Investing		$2.875 E	.500	
Coastal Corp.	B+	$ 1.83	1.000[b]	
Comdisco	B+	8.00 −03	27.397	
Commonwealth Edison	A−	$ 1.425	1.000	
Computer Sciences	B+	6.00 −94	37.040	
Computervision	B	8.00 −09	22.222	
Cooper Industries	A−	$ 2.90	.946	
CooperVision	NR	8.625	36.430	
Crown Zellerbach	B	$ 4.625 A	1.058	
Crown Zellerbach		$ 4.50 C	1.462	
Crown Zellerbach		9.25 −09	24.845	
Datapoint	B	8.875−06	12.048	
Deere & Co.	B+	5.50 −01	30.534	
Deere & Co.		9.00 −08	25.000	
Diamond Shamrock	B+	$ 4.00	1.228	
Digital Equipment	B+	8.00 −09	8.772	
Dominion Resources	A−	3.625−86	31.746	
Eastern Gas & Fuel	B	9.75 −08	33.003	
Eastman Kodak	A	8.25 −07	9.780	
Emerson Electric	A+	5.00 −92	22.381	6
ENSERCH	A	10.00 −01	35.014	
Federal National Mortgage Assn.	NR	4.375−96	50.942	
Financial Corp. America	B+	11.50 −02	68.182	
First Boston	B	9.25 −09	15.936	
Ford Motor	B	4.50 −96	24.000	7
Ford Motor		4.875−98	27.060	8
Freeport−McMoran	B+	10.50 −14	35.817	
GTE	A+	$ 2.50	.870	
GTE		4.00 −90	22.476	
GTE		5.00 −92	22.983	
GTE		6.25 −96	29.740	
GTE		10.50 −07	21.739	
General Instrument	B+	5.00 −92	49.432	

Company	Stock S&P	Convertible description	Conversion ratio[a]	End notes
Georgia Pacific	B+	5.25 −96	32.394	
Georgia Pacific		$ 2.24 A	1.000	
Georgia Pacific		$ 2.24 B	1.000	
Global Marine	B	$ 3.50	2.000	
Global Marine		13.00 −03	60.132	
Grace (W.R.) & Co.	B+	4.25 −90	17.446	
Great Western Financial	B−	8.875−07	32.786	
Greyhound	B+	6.50 −90	54.421	
Greyhound		6.00 −86	21.739	9
Hercules	B+	6.50 −99	28.571	
Hitachi Ltd. ADR	NR	5.75 −96	43.814[b]	
Holiday Inns	A	Series A	1.500	
Hospital Corp. of America	A+	8.50 −08	19.277	
Hospital Corp. of America		9.00 −98	15.117	
Household International	B+	$ 2.375	2.250	
Household International		$ 2.50	1.500	
Household International		$ 6.25	1.923	
Hughes Tool	B	9.50 −06	21.220	
Humana	A	8.50 −09	26.455	
ITT	B+	$ 4.00 H	1.884	
ITT		$ 4.50 I	1.696	
ITT		$ 4.00 J	1.698	
ITT		$ 4.00 K	1.631	
ITT		$ 2.25 N	1.266	
ITT		$ 5.00 O	1.447	
ITT		8.625−00	39.408	
Inexco Oil	B	8.50 −00	43.956	
International Business Machines	A+	7.875−04	6.508	
K mart	A−	6.00 −99	28.169	
Kaneb Services	B+	8.75 −08	57.000	10
LTV	C	Class AA	1.500	
LTV		$ 3.06 B	1.299	
LTV		$ 5.25 C	1.000[b]	
LTV		$ 1.25 D	1.220	
Lear Siegler	A−	$ 2.25	2.500	

Company	Stock S&P	Convertible description	Conversion ratio[a]	End notes
M/A-COM	B+	9.25 -06	27.397	
MAPCO	B+	10.00 -05	21.858	
McDermott International	B	$ 2.20	1.000	11
McDonnell Douglas	A	4.75 -91	32.667	
Merill Lynch & Co.	B+	8.875-07	31.873	
Mobile	A-	10.50 -08	25.000	12
Morgan (J.P.) Co.	A+	4.75 -98	25.000	
NBI	B-	8.25 -07	22.727	
NWA	B-	7.50 -07	19.704	13
National Medical Enterprises	A	9.00 -06	40.323	
National Medical Enterprises		12.625-01	36.075	
National Medical Enterprises		8.00 -08	29.586	
Occidental Petroleum	B	$ 3.60	3.237	
Occidental Petroleum		$ 4.00	3.155	
Occidental Petroleum		$ 6.25	1.250	
Owens-Corning Fiberglas	B	8.25 -07	26.230	14
Owens-Illinois	B+	$ 4.75	3.000	
Owens-Illinois		6.00 -92	33.898	
Paine Webber Group	B+	$ 2.25	.714	
Paine Webber Group		8.00 -07	23.364	15
Paine Webber Group		8.25 -08	18.889	
Pfizer	A+	4.00 -97	42.105	
Pfizer		8.75 -06	35.398	
Phelps Dodge	C	$ 5.00	1.818	
Pitney-Bowes	A	$ 2.12	2.000	
Pittston Co.	C	9.20 -04	20.000	
Pogo Producing	B	8.00 -05	25.316	
Pulte Home	B	8.50 -08	42.105	16
RCA	B+	$ 4.00	2.290	
RCA		$ 2.125	.714	
RCA		4.50 -92	17.844	
Ralston Purina	A+	5.75 -00	65.217	
Reading & Bates	B	$ 2.125	1.301	
Reynolds (R.J.)	A+	10.00 -08	15.936	17
Reynolds (R.J.)		10.00 -09	13.333	18

Company	Stock S&P	Convertible description	Conversion ratio[a]	End notes
Reynolds Metals	B	$ 4.50	2.131	
Reynolds Metals		4.50 −91	17.461	
Rockwell International	A+	$ 1.35	3.600	
Searle (G.D.) & Co.	A−	5.25 −89	22.748	19
Searle (G.D.) & Co.		4.50 −92	21.818	20
Signal Companies	B+	$ 4.125 A	1.471	21
Signal Companies		5.50 −94	27.717	
Singer Co.	B	9.00 −08	27.778	
Southwest Airlines	B+	10.00 −07	54.230	
Storage Technology	D	9.00 −01	27.211	
Storer Communications	B−	8.50 −05	25.000	22
Sun Co.	B+	$ 2.25	2.086	
Sybron	B+	$ 2.40	1.600	
TRW	A+	$ 4.40	2.200	
TRW		$ 4.50	1.862	
Tesoro Petroleum	B	$ 2.16	1.724	
Tesoro Petroleum		5.25 −89	59.172	
Textron	A−	$ 2.08 A	1.100	
Textron		$ 1.40 B	.900	
Tidewater	B+	7.75 −05	15.503	
Time	A−	$ 1.575 B	1.790	
Toys R Us	B+	8.00 −01	26.786	23
Transworld	NR	$ 2.00	.706	
Travelers	A−	$ 4.16 A	.975	
UAL	B	$ 2.40 B	.585	
Union Carbide	B	10.00 −06	15.180	
Union Pacific	A	$ 7.25 A	2.000	
Union Pacific		4.75 −99	69.979	
USAir Group	B+	$ 3.00 C	3.000	
USAir Group		8.75 −09	29.002	
United States Steel	B−	$12.75	4.494	
United States Steel		$ 2.25	.866	
United States Steel		5.75 −01	15.936	
United Technologies	A+	$ 2.55	.786	
Viacom International	A−	9.25 −07	29.762	

Company	Stock S&P	Convertible description	Conversion ratio[a]	End notes
Wal–Mart Stores	A+	$ 2.00 A	2.192	24
Walter (Jim)	B+	$ 1.60	1.350	
Walter (Jim)		5.75 −91	29.760	
Walter (Jim)		9.00 −07	33.557	
Wang Labs	A	7.75 −08	19.171	
Wang Labs		9.00 −09	30.418	
Western Union	C	$ 4.60	2.338	
Western Union		$ 4.90	2.610	
Western Union		5.25 −97	15.152	
Westinghouse Electric	A+	9.00 −09	32.258	
Weyerhaeuser	B	$ 2.80	1.212	
Weyerhaeuser		$ 4.50 A	1.111	
Woolworth (F.W.)	B	$ 2.20 A	1.420	
Xerox	A−	6.00 −95	10.870	

[1] Bond trades as Textron

[2] Bond trades as International Paper

[3] Bond trades as Sun Co.

[4] Bond trades as Chase Manhattan Bank

[5] Bond trades as Chemical Bank

[6] Bond trades as Skil Corp.

[7] Bond trades as Ford Motor Credit

[8] Bond trades as Ford Motor Credit

[9] Bond trades as Greyhound Computer

[10] Bond trades as Moran Energy

[11] Bond trades as McDermott Inc.

[12] Bond trades as InterNorth

[13] Bond trades as Northwest Airlines

[14] Bond trades as Corning Glass Works

[15] Bond trades as CIGNA

[16] Bond trades as Pulte Home Credit

[17] Bond trades as General Cinema

[18] Bond trades as General Cinema

[19] Bond trades as Will Ross

[20] Bond trades as Will Ross

[21] Trades as 8.25% preferred

[22] Bond trades as Storer Broadcasting

[23]Bond trades as Petrie Stores

[24]Trades as 8% preferred

[a]Conversion ratios are subject to change due to stock splits,etc.

[b]Convertible is exchangeable into a unit involving securities other than common stock.

Sources: Value Line Convertibles and Standard & Poor's .

TERMS APPLYING TO CONVERTIBLE SECURITIES AND OPTIONS

Accrued interest.   Interest earned on a bond since its last interest payment date. The buyer of the bond pays the market price plus accrued interest to the seller and is entitled to the next interest payment in full. Exceptions include bonds in default and income bonds, which are traded flat (without accrued interest).

Antidilution clause.   Provisions contained in most convertible indentures calling for adjustment of the conversion terms in the event of stock splits, stock dividends, or the sale of new stock at a price below the conversion price of existing convertibles. In some cases, no adjustment is made for small stock dividends (e.g. under five percent in any single year or ten percent during the life of the convertible).

Arbitrage.   See "Convertible arbitrage."

Beta.   A tool which measures the historical sensitivity of a stock's price movements to overall market fluctuations, useful in identifying market risk.

Bond Indenture.   The contract under which bonds are issued. It describes such terms of the agreement as interest rate, interest payment dates, date of maturity, redemption terms, conversion privileges, antidilution clauses, and the security for the loan.

Bond price quotation.   Bonds are quoted as a percentage of par. Thus, 90 represents 90 percent of a $1,000 bond, or $900. 110 means 110 percent of par, or $1,100.

Break-even time.   The time period necessary for a convertible bond or convertible preferred to recapture the premium paid over conversion value, via the extra income, when bond interest or preferred dividends exceed the common stock's dividend.

Call option.   An option granting the holder the right to purchase an asset at a specified price for a specified period of time.

Call price.   The amount of money a corporation is obliged to pay if it chooses to redeem its senior securities. In the case of bonds, the call price is usually expressed as a percentage of par. In the case of preferred stock, the call is the price per share. The call price is normally set somewhat above par and is reduced periodically.

Callable.   Term applying to securities whose indenture contains a provision giving the issuer the right to retire the issue prior to its maturity date.

Conversion parity.   The price at which the convertible must sell for it to equal the current market value of the common shares to be received upon conversion. If the convertible is trading at a premium above conversion parity, it is generally better to sell the convertible rather than to convert.

Conversion premium.   The difference between a convertible's market price and its conversion value expressed as a percentage above conversion value.

Conversion price.   The price at which the underlying common stock must trade in order for the bond to be worth par value if converted.

Conversion ratio.   The number of common shares to be received upon conversion.

Conversion value.   The worth of a convertible bond or preferred if it is converted into common stock. It is calculated by multiplying the number of shares to be received upon conversion by the current market price of the common.

Convertible arbitrage.   A simultaneous purchase and sale of related securities for an immediate profit upon conversion. This technique generally involves the purchase of a convertible bond or convertible preferred that is trading at a price below its conversion value, and the short sale of its common stock. The stock received from the conversion offsets the short sale.

Convertible bond.   A debt instrument exchangeable at the option of the holder into common stock or other securities in accordance with the terms of the bond indenture.

Convertible preferred stock.   An equity security, senior to the common stock, which may be exchanged at the option of the holder into common stock or other securities.

Convertible price curve.   A graph showing the expected convertible price for any stock price over the near-term future.

Convertible strategies line.   A graphical representation of risk-reward relationships for various investment strategies involving undervalued convertible securities.

Cumulative preferred.   A preferred stock which provides for payment of its omitted dividends (arrearages) before dividends may be paid on the company's common stock.

Current yield.   The interest or dividends paid annually by a company on a security, expressed as a percentage of the current market price of the security.

Default.   Failure of the bond issuer to meet a contractual obligation, such as payment of interest, maintenance of working capital requirements, or payment of principal via a sinking fund or at maturity.

Discounted bond.   A bond selling below par value.

Ex-dividend.   A preferred or common stock trading without its current dividend. A seller of the security on the ex-dividend date will receive the dividend.

Exercise price.   The price at which an option or warrant is exercisable. Also called the strike price.

Expiration of conversion privileges.   Termination date of a convertible's conversion privilege.

Fabricated convertible.   A combination of warrants plus bonds usable for exercise purposes at par value in lieu of cash.

Forced conversion.   Holders of convertibles may be forced to convert in order to capture conversion value if convertibles are called for redemption, if there is an adverse change in their conversion terms, or as an expiration date comes due.

Investment floor.   See "Investment value."

Investment value.   The estimated value of a convertible bond or convertible preferred stock without consideration of its conversion privilege. Also known as the investment floor.

Investment value premium.   The difference between a convertible's market price and its investment value expressed as a percentage above investment value.

Maturity date.   A fixed date when the company must redeem a bond by payment of the full face value to the bondholder.

Premium over conversion value.   See "Conversion premium."

Premium over investment value.   See "Investment value premium."

Profit profile.   A graphic presentation of a risk-reward analysis which permits a visual comparison of investment alternatives.

Put option.   An option granting the holder the right to sell an asset at a specified price for a specified period of time.

Redemption.   The act of retiring part or all of a bond issue prior to its maturity date. If a convertible bond issue is selling above the redemption price when it is called by the issuing company, redemption is equivalent to a forced conversion of the issue.

Registered bond.   A bond which is issued in the name of the holder. Interest is paid by check to the holder. Most convertible bonds are registered.

Risk-reward analysis.   A mathematical evaluation of a convertible relative to an appropriate combination of common stock and straight bonds used to identify undervalued investment alternatives.

Sinking fund provisions.   A requirement calling for the company to begin retiring a convertible issue prior to its maturity date.

Subordinated debenture.   A bond which is subject to the prior claim of other senior securities and usually not secured by any specific property.

Synthetic convertible.   Created by an investment in both warrants and money market instruments.

Undervalued convertible.   A convertible security having superior risk-reward characteristics relative to common stock and straight bonds, as determined by a risk-reward analysis.

Warrant.   A negotiable security issued by a company which represents a long-term option to purchase common stock from the company on specified terms.

Warrant agreement.   The contract under which warrants are issued.

Yield advantage.   The difference between the yield of a convertible and its underlying common stock.

Yield to maturity.   The effective yield of a bond, taking into account its premium or discount from par, if one holds it to maturity when it is expected to be redeemed by the company at par value.

The Convertible Funds

CLOSED-END FUNDS

American Capital Convertible Securities, Inc.
2777 Allen Parkway, Houston, Texas 77019
(713) 522-1111

Bancroft Convertible Fund, Inc.
42 Broadway, New York, N.Y. 10004
(212) 269-9236

Castle Convertible Fund, Inc.
75 Maiden Lane, New York, N.Y. 10038
(212) 480-0500

LOAD MUTUAL FUNDS

American Capital Harbor Fund, Inc.
2777 Allen Parkway, Houston, Texas 77019
(713) 522-1111

Convertible Yield Securities, Inc.
Eleven Greenway Plaza, Houston, Texas 77046
(713) 626-1919

Phoenix Convertible Fund
One American Row, Hartford, Ct. 06115
(617) 292-1000

Putnam Convertible Fund
One Post Office Square, Boston, Mass. 02109
(617) 292-1000

NO-LOAD MUTUAL FUNDS

Noddings-Calamos Convertible Income Fund
2001 Spring Road, Oak Brook, Illinois 60521
(800) 251-2411 outside Illinois
(800) 821-6458 within Illinois

Noddings-Calamos Convertible Growth Fund
2001 Spring Road, Oak Brook, Illinois 60521
(800) 251-2411 outside Illinois
(800) 821-6458 within Illinois

Index